AUDIT OF HABITS

AUDIT OF HABITS

Review, Refine, and Redesign Your Daily Routines

NAMITA BHALLA

NU VOICE
PRESS

NU VOICE PRESS

First published by NU VOICE PRESS 2025
An imprint of Hubhawks Pvt. Ltd
www.nuvoicepress.com

This is a work of fiction and all characters and incidents described in this book are the product of the author's imagination. Any resemblance to actual persons, living or dead, is entirely coincidental.

ISBN: 978-81-984189-6-8

Typeset by Saanvi Graphics, Noida
Printed at Manipal Technologies Limited, Manipal
Published by Nu Voice Press

To my father, Surinder Bhalla, who continues to bless us from beyond the heavens. Though he is not here to see this book come to life, I know he'd be proud of the journey that led me here.

Contents

The Daily Journey of Learning

Investing in Yourself
Amidst a Busy Corporate Life

LEARNING is a journey. Why don't we then use our journey to learn something new each day? I use my commute to work to listen to a podcast or a YouTube talk, something that's of interest and would help me in my journey of growth—whether in my professional or personal life.

In today's fast-paced corporate world, the idea of continuous learning often feels like a lofty goal rather than a realistic practice. Many of us lead extremely busy lives, managing tight deadlines, back-to-back meetings, and endless to-do lists. Believe me, being in auditing, I absolutely relate to having those insane days when getting up from the desk is also a luxury. Yet, it's essential to remember that learning doesn't have to require hours of our day. Instead, it can be integrated seamlessly into our daily routines, transforming those fleeting moments into opportunities for growth and investment in ourselves.

Why This Investment Matters?

Time is our most precious commodity, and investing it in learning can yield significant returns in our professional lives. Here are some real-life examples and strategies on how corporate professionals are making this investment work:

Short Learning Sessions

Consider Sarah, a senior project manager at a technology firm. She discovers that she can listen to short, impactful podcasts during her commute. By dedicating just twenty minutes each day, she enriches her knowledge on leadership and innovation. This small time commitment not only makes her commute enjoyable, but also equips her with fresh ideas that can be used in team meetings.

Micro-Learning Modules

Jason, a marketing director, attends multi-day conferences but finds that he often misses valuable insights due to time constraints. He starts allocating just ten minutes after lunch for micro-learning through online platforms which offer bite-sized courses relevant to his field. This allows him to stay updated with the latest marketing trends without overwhelming his schedule.

Utilising Breaks

Recognising her hectic schedule, Emily, a financial analyst, turns her coffee breaks into learning moments. She uses these brief periods to read industry reports or articles. Even a quick five to ten minutes read can sharpen her skills and keep her informed about market dynamics, directly impacting her performance.

Creating a Learning Circle

A group of busy executives at a consulting firm form a 'Learning Lunch' initiative, where they meet once a month during lunch hours to discuss a book or an article. This allows busy professionals to share insights and engage in thought-provoking discussions in an informal setting, all while enjoying their meals.

After-Hours Learning with Purpose

For those who find it challenging to carve out time during the workday, attending evening workshops or webinars can be a viable solution. Mark, a team lead, sets aside one evening each week to attend virtual workshops focused on skills like negotiation and emotional intelligence. This structured approach ensures that he continuously evolves without impacting his daily commitments.

Making the Commitment

Investing in your personal and professional development is an essential strategy for long-term success. Here's how you can start making learning a daily habit amidst your busy life:

- **Identify Gaps:** Reflect on areas you want to improve. Is it leadership, communication, or technical skills? Knowing what you want to learn helps in choosing the right content.
- **Choose Your Learning Method:** Whether it's podcasts, online courses, or books, select what fits seamlessly into your routine.
- **Schedule It:** Treat learning like a meeting on your calendar. Block time daily or weekly, even if it's just for ten to twenty minutes, and stick to it.
- **Be Flexible:** If your schedule changes, adapt your learning method accordingly. Try listening to audiobooks during your morning run or watching short videos while you take a break.

Incorporating learning into your busy life is not just feasible—it's essential. Remember, the best investment you can make is in yourself. By prioritising daily learning, you're equipping yourself not just to keep up with the ever-evolving corporate landscape, but to thrive in it.

Make the commitment today to invest a little time into learning daily. The insights you gain will create significant ripple effects in your career and personal life.

Happy learning!

Introduction

THIS isn't the first book written on the power and magic of habits, and wouldn't be the last either. However, it's a 1% investment in yourself, pushing you towards a 1% improvement each day—with each habit, with each page. Take just 1% of an hour, only six minutes, to read it, and join the rare 1% who lead healthier, happier lives and have peaceful routines.

No need to read this book in one go. Read it at your own pace, one habit or one story at a time. Reflect on and relish the life-changing story in each chapter, get inspired, and take a small step to bring a positive change in your life in whichever way possible for you. Your tiniest effort in this direction is more than enough.

The experiences narrated here are taken from my own life, along with those of people for whom these habits have worked miraculously, transforming them and their lives completely.

I have spent over a decade auditing financial accounts of companies and being a self-reflective person. Therefore, subconsciously, my profession also sneaked into my daily life. As I practiced these habits, a part of me also started auditing them, analysing the changes in my thinking patterns, reactions, responses, and persona.

* * *

What you will find here isn't something brand new and 'never heard of before.' It is simply a profound analysis of what is already there and known, its real-life impact and how to get started with implementing a 'known-new' habit. It is like performing a real 'audit' of these habits, i.e., dissecting them to understand what they are, their impact on our lives, what these habits can offer you if you choose to implement them, and how to practise them daily.

Habits are also contagious. Yes, they truly are. Pick any habit to start with and build a routine around it, and gradually you'll find other habits tagging along. If you start taking a ten-minute walk each day, a few days later you might find yourself spending another five to ten minutes just stretching or exercising a little. Gradually, you will become conscious of your eating habits and start drinking adequate amounts of water to stay hydrated.

An audit of habit is important not only to understand it better but to understand how that habit can suit you and serve your needs, desires, and wants. For example, waking up early is an ultimate habit we are encouraged to adopt and practise. But, if you work late nights since your job set-up is such, or work with clients in a different time zone, or if you are a student preparing for competitive exams and are more productive at night, then this habit might not suit you. But one takeaway from this habit could be—when you wake up, ensure you're in a peaceful environment. Then, spend the first few minutes just with yourself, without looking at any screens, because the way you start a day sets the tone for everything that follows. The quality of your day reflects the quality of your life.

* * *

Motherhood is a challenging journey. It gives mothers immense power to face and live each challenge. My motherhood journey was the point when I started to realise the importance of these habits. But the truth is to start as early as possible and not wait for something to give you a push. Be your own catalyst and give yourself that push to bring beautiful and remarkable changes in your lives. After all, the remote control of your life is in your hands. Operate it yourself, or else someone might control it without your knowledge. Sit in the driving seat of your life and follow a path that will lead to a successful, happy, and peaceful life. Hence, I started my efforts early while my child was still a toddler to introduce her to all these great habits and make them a part of her routine. It encompassed not just cleanliness, nutrition, and proper sleep but also mental and spiritual well-being, to make her today better than her yesterday.

Why did I realise about the importance of habits after being a mother?

Well, being concerned about the overall development of my baby from Day 1, I stumbled upon a lot of social media posts on early brain development and the right brain education. This intrigued me to know more about the subconscious mind and how it functions in the first few years, impacting our lives as grown-ups. The more I read about it and started to practise with my daughter, the more changes I could see in both of us. Hence, the audit of habits started.

Before this self-discovery journey, little did I know that my innate fears, low self-esteem, insecurities, and suppressed anger had its roots somewhere beyond my education and upbringing. It was in those years that I have little memory about. The initial years after my birth. No one really remembers that precious time, yet it has such a lasting impact on our lives. Of course, everyone around me cared for me. I was a happy child, loved by all. However, growing up wasn't easy. Love and happiness sometimes seemed to be diminishing with every passing year, even though it was not. It was just the expression of love that kept on diminishing. I was observant most of the times. My elders often told me that I was a 'quiet' child. I didn't know I was 'quiet'; I was just on 'observing' mode. But hearing my mother say this a couple of times, I became the 'quiet one'.

The 'quiet one' in the class, the 'quiet one' amongst friends, the 'quiet one' amongst cousins and relatives, and later on, the 'quiet one' in official meetings. Believing myself to be an introvert, I hardly made any special effort to make new acquaintances or friends.

I often found myself short of words at every occasion or gathering.

Habits, those silent architects of our lives, find their way into our subconscious minds, crafting the essence of who we become. The importance of habits became glaringly apparent to me during the crucial period of re-establishing routines, particularly when my daughter entered the scene after my maternity break.

The significance of these formative years, especially the first five, in shaping a person, cannot be overstated. They become imprinted in our character, influencing everything—from our emotional well-being to our approach to life's challenges.

My awakening to the power of habits was most pronounced when I had to construct a routine for my four-month-old daughter. Researching and integrating habits, spanning from gratitude to reading books, from daily water intake to nature walks, became a personal mission. Babies, being sensory learners, absorb from their environment. Hence, I embarked on the journey of integrating these habits into my own routine, recognising the potentially profound impact it could have on my child.

Almost anything can be transformed into a habit. The key is to start small, take it slowly, and be consistent. It will get embedded in your subconscious mind and gradually become automatic—like something you do by default. Once you understand and master this, success, happiness, and peace will become a habit. First, understand what your mind, body, and soul seek, and whether they are in sync.

Yoga

ONE of the foundational habits that transformed my life was yoga. So, what better way to begin this journey of habits than with yoga, the practice that starts our day?

John, a forty-two-year-old software developer, was struggling with severe back pain and high stress levels due to long hours of sitting and high job demands. After incorporating Hatha Yoga into his routine three times a week, John noticed significant improvements not only in his physical health—his back pain gradually diminished—but also in his mental health. His stress levels dropped, and his productivity at work increased.

The Origins and Evolution of Yoga

Yoga originated in the Indus-Sarasvati civilization in Northern India over 5,000 years ago. The word 'yoga' is derived from the Sanskrit root *Yuj,* which means to join or to unite, symbolising the union of body and consciousness. Initially a meditative and spiritual practice, yoga has evolved over centuries to include various styles and disciplines, each with its unique focus and techniques.

Yoga, a practice rooted in over 5,000 years of ancient Indian philosophy, has gained worldwide popularity as a holistic approach to health and well-being. Today, celebrities like Shilpa Shetty Kundra, and sports personalities like Sachin Tendulkar incorporate Yoga in their daily routines. Even business tycoons like Ratan Tata regularly practised and preached the habit of Yoga.

Never did I think I'd be doing yoga for my health. Making different postures and breathing exercises seemed boring and monotonous to me. But as soon as I got pregnant, I joined the pre-natal yoga classes in the seventh week itself. It turned out to be a great blessing for me and my child. It not only had a positive impact on my physical health but also on my emotional and spiritual health. I used to complain of shortness of breath before. After a few days of yoga, I never faced that problem again. I had a short temper, and the slightest of things could tick me off. However, during my entire pregnancy, I hardly had any mood swings. My husband was more amazed than me at this transformation. That was about my experience with yoga. Enumerating its endless benefits and the way it has changed most lives, it can be said that this truly is an essential habit to be imbibed in our daily routines.

Maria, a thirty-five-year-old breast cancer survivor, turned to yoga during her recovery phase. Engaging in gentle yoga sessions tailored for cancer survivors, Maria found tremendous relief from the side-effects of chemotherapy, such as fatigue and depression. The practice also provided her with a supportive community and a renewed sense of hope.

Scientifically-backed Benefits of Yoga

On Physical Health

- **Improved Flexibility and Balance:** Regular practice stretches and tones the body's muscles and improves its balance, reducing the risk of injury.
- **Enhanced Strength and Stamina:** Many yoga poses require sustaining body weight in different ways, which builds strength.
- **Better Breathing:** Techniques such as Pranayama (breath control) teach effective ways to breathe, enhancing lung function.

On Mental Health

- **Stress Reduction**: Yoga's emphasis on relaxation and meditation can help reduce stress and anxiety.
- **Improved Concentration and Mindfulness:** The practice encourages a focus on the present moment, which can improve overall cognitive function.

Spiritual Well-Being

- **Sense of Harmony and Peace:** The meditative aspects can help foster an increased sense of peace and calm.

Implementing Yoga into Daily Life

Getting Started

- **Choosing the Right Style:** It's important to choose a style that aligns with your physical capabilities and goals.
- **Finding a Qualified Instructor:** Ensure that the instructor is certified and experienced, particularly if you have health issues.

Creating a Routine

- **Frequency:** Beginners should aim for two to three sessions per week, gradually increasing the frequency.
- **Duration:** Start with shorter sessions of twenty to thirty minutes, and gradually increase as you become more comfortable.

Integrating Mindfulness and Meditation

- **Daily Meditation:** Begin or end your day with five to ten minutes of meditation to enhance the benefits of your yoga practice.
- **Mindful Breathing:** Use yogic breathing techniques throughout the day to maintain a calm and focused mind.

Yoga is more than just physical exercise; it is a comprehensive discipline that incorporates the mind, body, and spirit. The real-life examples of John and Maria illustrate how transformative and beneficial yoga can be, providing both healing and enhancing overall well-being. As we continue to explore and understand the depths of yoga's benefits, it becomes clear that this ancient practice holds modern-day relevance and potential for anyone seeking a healthier, more balanced life. Whether you are looking to heal physically, reduce stress, or find spiritual peace, yoga offers a path to achieving those goals.

If it hadn't been for Yoga, I would still be dealing with my impulsiveness, anxiety, and endless body aches. Making yoga a habit was the best decision for me, my daughter, and everyone around me.

Resources

1. Start with simple breathing exercises from YouTube.
2. Read *Adiyogi: The Source of Yoga* by Sadhguru.

Food for Thought

1. Have you done yoga before? If yes, do you see any noticeable changes in your life?
2. Jot down the changes you see in yourself before and after starting Yoga. Focus on both, your physical and mental health.
3. What are your key takeaways from this chapter?

More Than Just Mornings

IN the heart of Silicon Valley, where innovation never sleeps, there is one leader whose day starts earlier than most. Tim Cook, the CEO of Apple Inc., is not only known for leading one of the most valuable companies in the world but also for his unique personal habit—waking up early, at the ungodly hour of 3.45 a.m.

Tim Cook's journey into the early hours began long before he started to helm Apple. Raised in Robertsdale, Alabama, Cook learned the value of hard work and discipline from an early age. His early rising was initially more of a necessity than a choice, moulded by his upbringing and career demands. However, it soon became a cornerstone of his lifestyle, profoundly impacting his professional trajectory and leadership style.

A Day in the Life of Tim Cook

The quiet hours of the morning are crucial for Cook. This time is not about leisure; it's about gaining a head start on the world. His morning routine includes reviewing global

Apple operations and consumer feedback, which gives him insights into the company's daily pulse. He then moves on to email correspondence, sending out company updates and directives before most of his employees can hit the snooze button for the first time.

Cook uses his early hours to exercise, a practice that not only energises him but also sharpens his focus and resilience. By the time most executives are starting their day, Cook has already mapped out his priorities and strategies.

This habit of waking up early has been transformative for Cook and, by extension, for Apple. This proactive attitude allows him to address issues in real-time, maintain a hands-on approach to global markets, and foster a culture of responsiveness and accountability within the company. Under his leadership, Apple has seen the launch of ground-breaking products and services, navigating crises with agility and grace.

Tim Cook's transformation into a successful leader through his early rising habit is not just about gaining a few extra hours but the mind-set it fosters—a mind-set of anticipation, preparedness, and unmatched work ethic. As the world watches and learns, it becomes clear that sometimes, the key to unlocking potential could be as simple as setting the alarm clock a few hours earlier.

In the narrative of Tim Cook, the early morning hours are not just a part of the day; they are a pathway to innovation and excellent leadership.

This is one common habit amongst most successful people. They plan their mornings well and work effectively through their days. Having a fixed morning routine or ritual helps in clearing the mind and planning the day methodically. Whether the plan is to go for a run or have a peaceful time sitting in the patio with a cup of tea—sticking to it daily is essential for physical and mental fitness.

* * *

For the most of my schooling and higher studies, I was a night owl—always preferring to burn the midnight oil rather than getting up early. Although I got a good amount of peaceful study time, I felt depressed rising amidst the early morning chaos of the household. This left me irritated for the rest of the day. Even when my professional and married life started, I continued to be a night owl. Switching from a night owl to an early riser was a big task.

This meant that I had to first prepare my body for a proper sleep routine, so I could get tired early enough to get a good sleep and wake up fresh the next morning. Again, thanks to my daughter. I spent sleepless nights with her, feeding, rocking and playing till she was six months old. Then, I wanted her to get into a healthy sleep routine as well. It was a thoroughly enjoyable process of changing into her night clothes after dinner, reading her a bedtime story, kissing her goodnight, and then breast-feeding her to sleep. Her brain and body eventually got used to this process and automatically got the signal that it was night and she needed to sleep. Sometimes she woke up in the middle of the night out of hunger, but fell asleep again after taking her feed. When she woke up at 6 a.m., fresh and clear, I used to rise with her. After having my quick cup of tea, I accomplished a lot of tasks before starting for office than I used to do earlier, when I was a night owl. Besides, I felt positive and recharged in those calm morning hours. A morning routine is the best gift that I have received from my daughter.

The benefits of having a morning routine are innumerable, and it has an incredibly positive impact on our lives. There are endless books, articles, and talks on this. Though an age-old habit, it is still a hit with all the successful people. It's simple yet challenging, as it's not always easy to train your mind and body to leave the comfort of the warm, cosy bed. However, once you fall in love with the morning ritual, it's hard to stay in bed.

Benefits of Waking Up Early:

- You get more time to think and connect with yourself.
- You get better at problem-solving.
- There's more time to plan and organise your daily tasks.
- You get uninterrupted time to work in peace.
- It boosts mental health.
- There's more time to spend with your family.
- You get time to exercise, keeping several lifestyle diseases at bay.
- The extra hours grant peaceful study time, guaranteeing better grades.
- Finally, you feel positive and happier.

The list can go on and on as the benefits are endless, and each person experiences it uniquely. Implementing the habit of early rising can be transformative—enhancing productivity, focus, and overall well-being.

Tips to Adopt this Habit:

Set a Specific Goal

Determine why you want to wake up early. Whether it's for exercise, meditation, or uninterrupted work time, having a clear purpose can motivate you to stick with your new routine.

Gradually Adjust Your Schedule

If you're used to waking up at 8 a.m. but want to shift it to 5 a.m., gradually adjust the timing. Shift it fifteen to thirty minutes earlier every few days until you reach your target time.

Create a Relaxing Bedtime Routine

Develop a bed-time routine that signals to your body that it's time to wind down. This could include activities like reading, taking a warm bath, or meditating.

Optimise Your Sleep Environment

Ensure your bedroom is conducive to good sleep. This means having a comfortable mattress and pillows, blackout curtains, and a cool room temperature. Minimise noise and light disruptions.

Avoid Stimulants

Avoid caffeine and other stimulants in the late afternoon and evening. These can interfere with your ability to fall asleep.

Limit Screen Time Before Bed

The blue light emitted by screens can disrupt your natural sleep cycle. Try to turn off electronic devices at least an hour before bed.

Be Consistent

Stick to your rising time every day, even on weekends. Consistency reinforces your body's sleep cycle.

Use Technology Wisely

Consider using a sleep tracker to analyse your sleep patterns and a smart alarm to wake you up gently during your lightest sleep phase.

Prepare the Night Before

Lay out your clothes, arrange your breakfast ingredients, or organise your work materials the night before. Reducing morning stress can make waking up early more appealing.

Reward Yourself

Give yourself something to look forward to each morning. This could be a tasty breakfast, your favourite cup of coffee, or simply some quiet time to enjoy a hobby.

Evaluate and Adjust

Regularly assess how the new routine is affecting your health, mood, and productivity. Don't hesitate to tweak your schedule or strategy to suit your needs better.

Stay Motivated

Keep in mind the benefits you're aiming for, and remind yourself why you started. Tracking your progress can also provide motivation to keep going.

By incorporating these tips, you can make early rising a sustainable and beneficial part of your daily routine.

Resources

1. Read *The 5AM Club* by Robin Sharma.
2. Watch the morning routine video by Xiu House on YouTube: *A Peaceful Morning Routine of a Young Mother.*

Food for Thought

1. Have you ever tried waking up early?
2. If yes, how did you feel? What was the atmosphere like? What were nature's sounds like? How did you feel throughout the day—were you more in control, or did you rush through?
3. If not, do you want to put in the effort, if this improved the quality of your days and life?

THOUGHT BREAK

Motivation is a myth!

We often wait to feel motivated to pick up something new, work towards that goal, hit the gym, or take action on something that's outside of our comfort zone.

But does waiting help?

Never!

Motivation is not going to ring the doorbell.

Your wait is going in vain.

What helps, then?

Taking action.

Action precedes motivation.

When you force yourself to get up and start exercising, you feel motivated.

When you pick up a book and read a page, you feel motivated to read more.

Ask a student who doesn't like to study but does it anyway before the exams. He is not motivated, but the exam deadline forces him to pick up the book.

If it helps, keep a deadline for yourself to force you into action.

So, don't wait to start. Just start instead. Motivation will follow.

Motivation is a by-product of action, not the spark.

Ever noticed that when you are in a bad mood, the food you make senses it and gets spoilt?

Yes, it happened with me.

The other day, my mind was overflowing with numerous thoughts–some made me anxious, stressed, and worried, while some made me a little hasty.

The outcome? A burnt toast and a cup of tea that tasted bitter.

I had it anyway, because I didn't have the time or patience to make it again.

But don't you think that if food can feel our mood, our work can feel it too?

If our food can get spoilt, so can our work.

Our mood influences

- Productivity
- Creativity
- Decision-making
- Collaboration

When we're

- Stressed, anxious, or worried, our work suffers
- Positive, focused, and calm, our work thrives

The energy we emit impacts

- Team dynamics
- Client relationships
- Problem-solving

To protect your work from your mood

- Take breaks to clear your mind
- Prioritise self-care
- Practise mindfulness

Remember

You are the ingredient that makes your work exceptional.

The Art of Reading

I WENT to an Anglo-Indian school as a child. One of the best things about it was that every academic prize winner was given a novel on the prize distribution day. I was too much into academics and hardly read anything for pleasure. As a result, I didn't have a reading habit either. Had it not been for those prizes which I won for academic excellence, I wouldn't have explored any books. I started with *The Jungle Book* (the first book I won as a prize) and then read endless fiction pieces. After reading *The Secret*, I added many non-fiction books to my mini library too. It was that reading habit which made me more aware and provided a window to the world. Being from a humble middle-class family, travelling was a luxury we didn't have easy access to. It was this habit that eventually gave birth to the journaling or writing habit that I have. And sooner or later, writing became a passion and led me to write more professionally and publish my work. All of this was a result of that childhood reading habit.

Reading is a habit every successful and established person has. Often related to introverts, this forms a part of extroverts' routines as well. Books, whether fiction or non-fiction, provide you with a whole new perspective. I was surprised to know that this is a habit we can inculcate in our babies right after their birth. Reading with my little one is truly the best way to end each day. I've hardly come across any successful professional who doesn't have a reading list.

Reading books like *101 Ways to be a Stress-free Mom and Raise Happy Kids* by Lahar Bhatnagar have also helped me deal with life smartly. They came as a saviour when I was anxious and depressed as a new mom. I realised I was not alone in this situation and learned tips and tricks from the real-life experiences of those who had been through this phase.

Recently, Booklet Guy (also known as Amrut Deshmukh) has been gaining popularity for his Booklet app. His love for reading was so profound that his mission statement was 'Make India Read'. Through his app, he published summaries of books we always wanted to read but couldn't, owing to our busy and demanding lifestyles. Hence, his app helped people reap the benefits of the books in the least amount of time. Later, he went a step further to deliver book summaries in audio format, making it more convenient for people to catch up on their favourite books and authors.

* * *

Sudha Murty, the Chairperson of Infosys Foundation and a prolific Indian author, stands out as a beacon of inspiration, illustrating the transformative power of reading. Her journey from growing up in a simple, middle-class family in Karnataka to becoming one of India's most respected philanthropists and writers is a testament to the profound impact that the habit of reading can have on an individual's life.

Early Encounters with Literature

Sudha Murty's passion for reading was ignited in her childhood, thanks to her grandfather who was a school teacher. He introduced her to the world of books, starting with the Indian epics, Mahabharata and Ramayana, and later to other forms of literature. This early exposure to a variety of texts shaped her understanding of the world and honed her empathy.

Engineering a Path Through Books

As one of the first female engineers to study at the Indian Institute of Engineering in Hubli, Sudha Murty often turned to books as a source of comfort and guidance. Reading was not only a refuge but also a means of expanding her horizons beyond the technical world. Her diverse reading habits included works of fiction, non-fiction, science, philosophy, and history, which broadened her perspectives and deepened her understanding of human nature.

The Influence of Reading on Career and Philanthropy

Sudha Murty's extensive reading habit influenced her approach to both her professional life and her philanthropic activities. As she transitioned from a computer scientist and engineer to a writer and social worker, her insights from books helped her address various social issues such as healthcare, education, and poverty alleviation. Her literary works often reflect themes of common human values, kindness, and the importance of giving back, which are also central to her philanthropic vision.

Writing as an Extension of Reading

Sudha Murty's writing career is a direct extension of her reading habit. She has authored numerous books, ranging from children's literature to adult fiction and non-fiction, drawing heavily from her personal experiences and the stories she had encountered in her readings. Her books are celebrated for the simplicity with which they discuss complex themes, making profound philosophical and ethical insights accessible to all ages.

Legacy and Ongoing Impact

Through her foundation and her writings, Sudha Murty continues to inspire the new generation about the importance of reading and education. Her work emphasises that reading not only enhances knowledge and personal growth but also fosters empathy and a commitment to social justice.

A Lifetime of Learning

Sudha Murty's story underscores the transformative power of reading. It shows how books can guide one's career path, inspire philanthropic endeavours, and lead to a fulfilling life of giving and writing. Her journey from a curious reader to a leader in social change exemplifies how lifelong learning can create a profound impact, not just on the individual but also on society at large.

Practical Tips to Cultivate a Reading Habit

Implementing a reading habit can be beneficial for people from all walks of life, whether they are children, parents, corporate professionals, entrepreneurs, or homemakers. Here are some simple, practical tips tailored for each group to help cultivate a love for reading:

For Children

- **Create a Reading Space:** Designate a special corner in your home as a reading nook. Make it cosy with cushions, good lighting, and easy access to books.
- **Set a Routine:** Incorporate reading into the daily routine, perhaps before bedtime or after dinner, to establish consistency.
- **Lead by Example**: Let your children see you read. Children who see adults engaged in reading are more likely to pick up the habit themselves.
- **Interactive Reading:** Make reading interactive by discussing the story, asking questions, and connecting events in the book to real-life experiences.
- **Library Visits:** Regular visits to the library can turn into an exciting adventure for children as they get

to choose new books and participate in reading programs.

For Parents

- **Read Aloud:** Regardless of the child's age, read aloud to them. This can strengthen relationships and improve literary, hearing, and speaking skills.
- **Book Choices:** Allow children to pick books they are interested in to keep them engaged.
- **Discuss What You Read:** Share what each family member is reading over dinner. This promotes interest and discussion about different topics.
- **Set Reading Goals:** Set achievable reading goals as a family and celebrate when they are achieved, perhaps with a special meal or a family outing.

For Corporate Professionals

- **Audiobooks and Podcasts:** Utilise commuting or travel time by listening to audiobooks or literary podcasts.
- **Reading Breaks:** Replace some digital breaks with short reading sessions. Even 10–15 minutes can be refreshing and informative.
- **Professional Development:** Incorporate books that align with your career goals.
- **Book Clubs:** Start or join a book club at work to encourage reading and discussion among colleagues.

For Entrepreneurs

- **Industry-relevant Books:** Focus on books that provide insights into your industry, emerging trends, and business strategies.
- **Biographies for Inspiration:** Read biographies of successful entrepreneurs to find inspiration and learn from their experiences.
- **Schedule Reading Time:** Block out time in your calendar for reading as you would for any important business meeting.
- **Leverage Summaries:** For efficiency, use book summaries and reviews to decide which books might be most beneficial before diving in.

For Homemakers

- **Join a Library:** Make use of local library resources to explore a variety of genres without the expense of buying books.
- **E-Books and Online Resources:** Utilise e-books and online platforms for easy access to a vast array of reading materials.
- **Social Reading Apps:** Use apps like Goodreads to track reading progress, set challenges, and connect with other readers.
- **Read in Small Slices:** Fit reading into your schedule in small chunks, while waiting for appointments or during breaks in your daily routine.

By tailoring the approach to fit the lifestyle and interests of each group, reading can become a more integrated and enjoyable part of daily life.

* * *

Shanaya had been dealing with depression and attempted suicide when she was eighteen—her entire life still waiting to be explored. Yet, she had lost all interest in life. For someone who had always been chirpy, cheerful, and full of life, this was extremely hard. She loved to travel and explore the beauty of nature. During one of her college exploration trips, she had met someone special and got into a relationship soon after. She called him her exploration buddy. Deeply in love, she hadn't the slightest notion of what life had in store for her next. Her exploration buddy went for a mountaineering trip and met with an accident, losing his life. It was tragic for that guy and his family, but Shanaya couldn't bring herself to find peace with this reality either. She went through a number of counselling sessions before she could force herself to sit down with a book on her counsellor's advice. She found relief in *Man's search for Meaning* by Victor E. Frankl. Then she went on to read *The Ultimate Gift* by Jim Stovall and found a new perspective to life. It would be right to say that reading not only saved her life but gave her a rebirth. Thereafter, she went back to her exploration life and started learning photography to capture nature's beauty in frames. However, a book always found its way in her travelling bag as a forever companion.

While doing my research, I stumbled upon an article by Saurabh Jain, the Vice President of Paytm, where he mentioned that he started reading books as a regular habit in January 2015—his aim being to read one book per week. In three and a half years, he had read over 160 books. Jain said, 'In the first year, nothing much changed externally, but I began to change internally. I became happier and more positive. In next two and a half years, I became the Vice President of Paytm (one of India's largest unicorn start-ups) and a speaker at multiple conferences, including the prestigious SXSW Edu conference.'

Resource

1. Follow Jim Kwik, an American coach and podcaster, for his quick reading techniques.
2. Explore the Booklet App.

Call to Action

Pick any book, article, or newsletter of interest and start reading it for five minutes each day. Keep these five minutes consistent.

Food for Thought

1. Have you ever picked up a book that interested you and got hooked to it?
2. How was the experience of reading? What were your takeaways from that book?
3. If you could develop any skill just by reading about it, what would it be? Are there any books on this?

You're Your Own Friend

JOURNALING—THE habit that made me write this book. It is what made me write my heart out in a journal while my daughter was in my womb, and I still continue to do that. I write everything I feel for my daughter in that journal—her milestones, the joys and feelings I want to share with her, and everything positive around her. It's like capturing the life around her in words.

This is a great way to vent your emotions, stay close to your goals, record your progress each day, and feel lighter once you write it out. Journaling is that keystone habit that can change you for the better and impact every area of your life. It is also a way to re-live life's best experiences. It has helped me discover my creative self and understand the true essence of creativity, which is not restricted to just the art forms. It can be present everywhere if we choose to think creatively. It's about finding creative solutions to our problems and imbibing them in our tasks.

Josh Waitzkin, author of *The Art of Learning*, wakes up and immediately writes in his journal for thirty minutes.

Another budding fiction author, Kavya Sharma, the author of *All Seasons Alike*, once wrote on her Instagram account that the first thing she does after waking up in the morning is writing in her journal. She writes whatever comes to her mind, and she makes it a point to include everything positive. This gives a great start to her day, fostering a feeling of fulfilment.

According to Robin Sharma, the author of *The Monk Who Sold His Ferrari*, your day is your life in miniature—a great thought to stimulate you to make your days better. Rather than escaping reality by spending time scrolling through social media accounts and checking e-mails every now and then, it's better to capture the morning creative bursts by penning them down. Now, whether it's during the morning journal session or in the evening after winding up the day's work—this habit will help crystallise your creativity and goals. It will help you see what you really need to include in your life and days, and what needs to be deleted or reduced. **Design the life you wish to live**, and as the author and creator of your own life story, get as creative as you want and go beyond limits to see the magic unfold.

What is also crucial is to write by hand. The feel of pen and paper connects with the brain's motor cortex and is equivalent to meditation.

* * *

Let me tell you a story.

Sapna was an exceptionally quiet and reserved child at school. Afraid of public speaking, she did not participate in any single extra-curricular activity, seeking refuge in books instead. She had a secret journal where she poured out her thoughts, the paper a patient listener and her closest friend. She ranted and shared over and over again on the pages without the fear of being judged. She re-visited her entries after every few months, recollecting and reflecting upon what she had been thinking in the past, and in the process gained emotional maturity, getting to know her strengths and weaknesses. When she grew up, she became immensely creative not only at writing but also at her accounting job. Yes, something as monotonous as accounts can go hand in hand with creativity. She offered creative accounting solutions to her company's higher management and made her way to the top—a completely different person from her childhood self. Though still a woman of few words, putting them across creatively had helped her make great friendships and relationships too. Years after, she became a CFO and a successful business blogger. How did journaling help her achieve this? Writing about her deepest desires, life goals, and dreams kept her motivated and helped carve out a path leading to the life she wanted to live. This is where the universal law of attraction also works. Attracting the forces of the universe towards your goals and working towards them; grabbing the opportunities as they come your way. Her daily to-do list journal was in line with her long-term goals, and a tick mark on her daily to-do tasks inched her closer to the goals she envisioned.

This gave her time for self-care. A perfect, timely disconnect from work and scribbling her thoughts and even poetry at times helped her strike the required balance in life. A post-work reflection time made her less stressed and more content. It also developed strong writing habits and made her an effective communicator. It cleared her mind and crystallised her ideas.

Journaling ingrained the habit of gratitude in her life. She was thankful for everything she had and even encouraged gratitude in others. Being grateful towards life has its own benefits. It makes one happier, helps win friends and build a career, strengthens emotions, infuses optimism, develops personality, reduces envious feelings, improves decision-making, increases productivity, helps to relax, improves sleep, and so on. The list is infinite.

How to Implement this Habit?

- Include it in your morning ritual or at bed time.
- Consciously practise gratitude by writing down and being grateful for every good thing in life.
- Just write for yourself. No one else needs to read your journal, so write away all your thoughts—whatever comes to mind. It need not be in perfect grammar.
- Write every day for at least a month to make it a habit.
- Take action on the goals you have written. Make conscious efforts towards them.
- Re-visit your writings every now and then. This will just help you reflect more.
- Listen to music when you write. It helps.

Food for Thought

1. What are some thoughts you want to put down on a paper? How does that make you feel?
2. Have you ever written down your goals? (Fact: You get closer to your goals the more you read them.)
3. Would you want to make journaling a habit if that helps you be more productive and in control of your emotions?
4. Imagine if each day of the year could be a page in a book—would you author this book of 365 pages, filling it with your experience of each day?

THOUGHT BREAK

The Power of Passion Projects!

Have you ever worked on something that made time irrelevant?

When passion takes over, hours fly by unnoticed. Day turns to night, and exhaustion fades away.

That's the magic of working on something you truly care about.

Passion projects

- Energise, not drain
- Inspire, not exhaust
- Motivate, not bore

External factors fade away

- Hunger, thirst, and fatigue disappear
- Self-doubt and fear lose grip
- Creativity and innovation thrive

Invest in a passion project to

- Reignite your spark
- Discover new purpose
- Unlock hidden potential

Or, infuse passion into your current work

- Find meaning in your tasks
- Connect with your 'why'
- Drive impact, not just output

Remember

- Time is relative; passion, absolute.

Are you in a dilemma right now?

It's always a conflict to live in dilemma.

Dilemma of choosing between Commerce, Arts, and Science in school

Dilemma of choosing a college and a professional course

Dilemma of choosing the right life-partner

Dilemma of choosing the right job and company

Dilemma of stepping into motherhood or not.

Dilemmas are always going to be there.

It's not about making the right choice, but more about making your choice right with your efforts and dedication.

No choice is perfect, but every choice leads to growth.

Your experiences shape your perspective, so trust yourself and take the leap.

'That's a wrong career choice!'

'Marrying that person would be the worst decision!'

'This investment will never pay off!'

We do this all the time. We judge others' decisions and sometimes call them outright crazy.

Why?

Because we see them through our own lens.

Because we assess them as per our exposure to and experience of the world.

But what about the actual decision makers' lens? Their exposure and experience?

They're certainly not crazy but have a different lens than ours.

We should just observe and acknowledge that.

Ignorance is Bliss?

'IGNORANCE is bliss' is a phrase coined by Thomas Gray in his 1768 poem "Ode on a Distant Prospect of Eton College". The poet nostalgically reminisces about the carefree days of playfulness while young, oblivious about the dark realities of adult life. The poem reveals Gray's double perspective that not only is ignorance bliss, but knowledge is misery. Ignorance is bliss only when used in a way to remain grounded and avoid unnecessary problems. Related mostly to childhood like in Gray's poem, it is a blissful period of life full of innocence. One very practical sentence I came across during my research was 'Ignorance keeps human interactions healthy. It's good to be ignorant in this fast-changing world. To survive, human touch is more essential than any kind of information.' I couldn't agree more with the valuable truth hidden in this sentence.

There is only one way to avoid criticism as Aristotle said, 'Do nothing, say nothing, and be nothing'. Many times, in our lives, we come across unpleasant comments. At times, these require a reply. However, most of the times, it's better to ignore and avoid getting into arguments. It's a waste of time and energy. Ignoring things that are not worthy of our attention helps us lead peaceful lives. This the shortest route to peace in most situations. It saves us the unnecessary energy and efforts spent in useless arguments to prove a point that doesn't even matter after some time.

However, having said all of this, you should not be ignorant of facts and common knowledge, as that can be harmful to both yourself and others.

Tune out nonsense. Focus on what matters.

It's best to ignore situations and small talks that don't really deserve a reaction from you. When you know that a reaction would be a complete waste of time and energy, choose to ignore it. Prioritise your peace over everything else.

When it comes to your goals and innovation, at times it is good to ignore the negativity and pessimism around because people try to impose their traditional ideas and experiences. But if you have the boldness and courage to ignore negativity and reinvent new structures, go ahead like Dr Verghese Kurien.

Dr Kurien, known as the 'Father of the White Revolution' in India, spearheaded the world's largest dairy development program, Operation Flood. Despite having no prior experience in dairy farming, his ignorance of the traditional methods and scepticism allowed him to innovate freely. He focused on empowering local farmers with cooperative structures and modern techniques. This approach led to the transformation of India from a milk-deficient nation to the largest milk producer in the world, significantly improving the livelihoods of millions of farmers. His ignorance of the 'impossibility' of such a massive transformation proved to be a blissful advantage, leading to unprecedented success.

Tips to Practise to Ignore Negativity

Differentiate between Constructive and Destructive Criticism

- Learn to distinguish between constructive feedback, which can help you grow, and destructive criticism, which is meant to bring you down. Focus on the former and disregard the latter.

Set Boundaries

- Establish clear boundaries with people who tend to be overly critical or negative. Limit your interactions with them to protect your mental peace.

Practise Mindfulness

- Engage in mindfulness practices such as meditation or deep breathing exercises. These can help you to stay grounded and be less affected by negative comments.

Positive Affirmations

- Use positive affirmations to reinforce your self-worth and capabilities. Remind yourself of your strengths and achievements regularly.

Surround Yourself with Positivity

- Spend time with supportive and positive individuals who uplift and encourage you. Their positive energy can counterbalance any negativity you encounter.

Focus on Your Goals

- Keep your goals and aspirations at the forefront of your mind. When you are focused on what you want to achieve, it becomes easier to ignore distractions and negativity.

Limit Social Media Exposure

- Social media can be a breeding ground for negativity. Limit your time on these platforms and curate your feed to include positive and inspiring content.

Develop a Thick Skin

- Understand that not everyone will agree with or support you. Accept that criticism is a part of life and learn to let it roll off your back without taking it personally.

Seek Professional Help

- If negative chatter or criticism significantly impacts your mental health, consider seeking help from a therapist or counsellor. They can provide strategies and support to help you cope.

So, let's take control and decide what we allow into our lives and what we choose to ignore, be it negative chatter, unwanted criticism, or unpleasant verbal attacks.

Food for Thought

1. Have you ever been in a situation that blew out of proportion because of someone's impulsive reaction?
2. What would you choose to ignore if it could give back your peace of mind, time, and energy?

Cleanliness is Next to Godliness

MANISHA was a worried mother. A mother is a natural worrier somehow—maybe the relationship is such. The cause of her worry was her son Aveer's deteriorating academic performance. She sensed his lack of concentration and focus. She tried teaching him herself, arranged some professional tutors, and even encouraged peer studies. Despite the efforts, there wasn't much change in the results. One fine morning, she came across an article in the 'Lifestyle' section of the newspaper. It was about organisation. She paused and reflected for a moment on her surroundings. She realised she had been so engrossed in her duties and worries as a mother that she seldom decluttered her son's room, organising it in a way that would give him more space.

One Sunday morning, she took up the task of decluttering and organising his entire room, right from his wardrobe to his study space. Aveer was confused at first as to what had gotten into his mother. Later, he offered to help when he saw her doing it so passionately for his sake. This worked wonders for Manisha as she saw the multi-layered benefits that followed. That activity enhanced her bond with Aveer. He started to share his feelings and thoughts with Manisha more candidly. Gradually, he grew conscious enough to keep his room neat and tidy, cleaning it daily. This was because he had himself contributed to the efforts in organising and re-arranging it. He now had more space on his study table, and an organised book-shelf saved time in finding the right book at the right time.

He subconsciously introduced the concept of organisation to his study time as well—he started making neater notes while studying, organising them with bookmarks and sticky notes. His self-study time and concentration span increased slowly. Slowly, Aveer even discovered his fondness for certain subjects and his grades improved in the next term. Manisha had never thought even in her wildest dreams that a simple act of organisation would have such a deep-rooted impact. She now had one less thing to worry about.

* * *

Everyone enjoys space and so does our mind. It is more productive when there is no clutter around and a lot of free space. Ideas start to flow in, and one starts respecting and valuing their time. Even a computer is more efficient when we keep the desktop clean and delete all the temporary and unnecessary files. Many times I've noticed that I'm in an awful mood when things are unorganised and messy. As a child, I didn't know the reason for my irritation. As I grew up and realised why, it became automatic and natural for me to declutter any space I'd be in. The smallest of changes caused bigger transformations in me. As I got up every morning, my first work was to make my bed. This small habit made a huge impact on my days.

Clutter reduces your productivity and makes you feel overwhelmed. Organising your space gives you time to focus on more important tasks, thereby increasing productivity. I personally love to keep my bathroom organised, even beautifying it with indoor plants and flowers. Also, having some great floral fragrances in that space rejuvenates my mood greatly. Bathroom is our private space—where we visit the first thing in the morning as we get out of the bed. Making it aesthetically appealing naturally uplifts one's mood in the morning. Being the ultimate private space, it is the place where I get most of my writing inspirations and professional ideas. I have often written blogs while in the bathroom, scribbling a rough version on my phone's Notes app as soon as the idea strikes. Organisation is so relevant to our lives that we have a booming industry of professional organising coaches helping people organise their homes and work spaces. The market is full of products and hacks, ranging from tiny clips to massive organiser wardrobes.

* * *

Marie Kondo, a Japanese organising consultant, author, and TV presenter made her entire career around this habit of tidying up. She got into the habit of tidying up when she was only five, after seeing her mother practicing Feng Shui. As per Kondo, 'The house was not tidy enough to have the Feng Shui effect.' As a result, Kondo began implementing the 'tidying up' process at such a tender age to help out her mother. Who knew that her passion for tidying spaces would not only be her career, but also get her to the TIME 100 list of the world's most influential people!

How to Implement the Organising Habit?

- Write down the tasks you need to do or make lists and revisit them until all of them are accomplished.
- Prioritise.
- Make schedules and keep realistic deadlines.
- Act on it or Do it now (follow the 'it's either now or never' philosophy).
- Designated a place for everything (what's important here is to keep things back in their respective places immediately after use).
- Declutter regularly (follow a minimalistic approach).
- Delegate responsibilities. At home, make other family members responsible for a few spaces. At work, create a structure that requires everyone to take ownership of their space, tidying them regularly.
- Spend less time on gadgets.

Resource

1. Watch Marie Kondo's shows, *Tidying Up with Marie Kondo* and *Sparking Joy with Marie Kondo*, on Netflix.

Food for Thought

1. How do you feel when you enter a hotel lobby—clean, spacious, well-organised, and fragrant? Would you want to create that space for your home and office too?
2. How do you feel when you are working on a cluttered desk versus a clean desk?

THOUGHT BREAK

How quickly can you become a billionaire?

In our fast-paced corporate world, we often set ambitious goals and expect rapid results. But nature teaches us that transformation happens slowly with consistent effort and patience.

A seed becomes a tree over twenty years with daily care. A caterpillar transforms into a beautiful butterfly gradually.

Let's apply this wisdom to our personal and professional growth. When we set large goals, we must remember that the journey prepares us for success.

Shed off impatience and embrace the gradual process of self-investment. Focus on daily progress, not instant gratification.

Remember, the time in between goals is not a delay, but a preparation. It's when the real growth happens.

So, let's celebrate small wins, learn from failures, and trust the process.

The best thing in life is to do the work you love.

Well, sometimes that's not a possibility for all of us, given what life throws at us at different stages.

The second-best thing in life is to love the work that you do.

This is something that can be made a possibility in every situation.

Change the lens and look at the silver lining.

Change 'complaint mode' to 'gratitude mode'.

Let go of what's out of your control and keep doing what's within your influence.

Perfect your Workspace

EVER walked into your office and felt like you were stepping into a scene from a chaotic sitcom—papers flying everywhere, coffee mugs with mysterious origins, and a laptop that's one notification away from a meltdown! We've all been there, and it's not pretty. Let's dive into the art of perfecting your workspace with a sprinkle of humour and a dash of Marie Kondo magic.

Marie Kondo's Influence on Workspaces

Marie Kondo has revolutionised the way we think about organisation with her KonMari Method. Her approach isn't just for the home—it's perfect for workspaces too. By keeping only what truly adds value, the method helps to create a space that supports your goals and well-being. Many have found that applying her principles to their workspace has led to increased focus and a sense of calm.

Why Bother Organising?

Imagine trying to cook a gourmet meal in a kitchen where you can't find the spatula. Frustrating, right? The same goes for your workspace. A clutter-free environment isn't just about aesthetics; it's about creating a space where your mind can focus and your creativity can flourish. Studies have shown that a well-organised workspace can boost productivity and reduce stress. So, let's roll up those sleeves and get to work!

Desk Setup: The Foundation of Productivity

Your desk is the heart of your workspace. Here's how to make it a powerhouse of efficiency:

- **Ergonomics Matter:** Ensure your chair supports your back, your screen is at the eye-level, and your feet rest flat on the ground. Your body will thank you.
- **Declutter:** Keep only essential items on your desk. Think minimalist—a lamp, a notebook, a pen holder, and maybe a plant for some greenery.
- **Cable Management:** Use cable organisers to keep those pesky wires in check. Trust me, untangling cables is no one's idea of fun.

Digital Organisation: Taming the Virtual Jungle

Our digital workspace can be as chaotic as our physical one. Here's how to keep it tidy:

- **Email Inbox Zero:** Aim to clear your inbox daily. Use folders and labels to categorise emails. Barack Obama was known for his disciplined email habits—if he can do it, so can you!
- **File Management:** Create a logical folder structure and stick to it. Regularly delete or archive files you no longer need.
- **Desktop Clean-up:** A cluttered desktop reflects a cluttered mind. Keep only current projects on your desktop and file away the rest.

Daily Routines: Small Habits, Big Impact

Incorporate these routines into your daily life to maintain an organised workspace:

- **Start and End Clean:** Begin and end your day by tidying up your desk. It sets a positive tone for the day and provides closure.
- **Digital Detox:** Set aside time each week to organise your digital files and clear out unnecessary emails.
- **Marie Kondo's Magic:** Apply her famous question, 'Does it spark joy?' to your workspace. If an item doesn't serve a purpose or bring you joy, it's time to let it go.

This really worked for me when my responsibilities at work had increased drastically with higher level management roles. Being responsible for multiple critical projects means you can be pulled from all directions at any given point. Without having a proper process, organised structure, and fool-proof plan in place, this almost definitely means disaster. This is where having organised files on your desktop, planned to-do lists, and some space for clarity come to be of great help.

Call to Action

Ready to transform your workspace? Start with one small change today. Whether it's clearing off your desk or organising your digital files, every step counts. Your future self will thank you!

Food for Thought

1. Have you tried perfecting your workspace before? Did you notice any significant changes in yourself after doing so?
2. Reflect on your productivity while working at a messy desk versus a clean and organised one.

All Work and No Play?

WE owe exercise to our bodies. A good exercise for the body will in turn make us active and happy after releasing endorphins. Fitting this into our daily routines makes us accomplish more tasks during the day. It helps in shrugging off the unwanted laziness. Valuing the body that we have and maintaining it with exercise is our duty. If you get your body moving, your life gets moving. That's the clear mantra. Exercise doesn't only have an impact on the way you look but also on the way you feel about yourself and your performance at work.

Rujuta Diwekar, a renowned dietician, often says in her books that weight loss shouldn't be the goal of people's lives. Rather, the goal should be having a healthy lifestyle and balanced eating habits. If you're exercising just to shed those extra kilos, you might lose track and discontinue after not seeing immediate results. However, if one makes exercising an integral part of their routine, they will feel its impact in all their activities. The habit of exercising will help you to kick out all the bad habits you have, especially unhealthy eating habits, or at least reduce their frequency greatly. Exercising has time and again helped people not only physically but also mentally and emotionally. The release of endorphins can have a deeper impact than one can imagine.

* * *

Sam was in his early twenties when he lost his father to a severe disease. Losing him at a time when he was still figuring out a career for himself was devastating and left him clueless about how to support his widowed mother and younger siblings. While he took up an entry level back-end process job at an IT company to run the household, he was internally disturbed and couldn't share his true feelings with anyone. He had no close friends with whom he could share his grief and the challenges he was going through. Slowly he started feeling frustrated, stressed, anxious, irritated, depressed, and clueless about life.

He went to the gym in his office on one of the days when he was a little less occupied at work and started running on the treadmill and did a twenty minutes' workout. He felt a little relieved and less anxious after the run. He did that again the next day and felt better after—less anxious and depressed—and was able to get a better sleep as well. Slowly, he started increasing his time on the treadmill and even started a few weight exercises, slowly increasing his time each week. With each sweat, he felt he was able to release the grief of his father's loss which he often avoided doing through tears, hence finding an alternative outlet for the grief. He went on to run a 5000 kilometre, followed by a 10,000, and then a half marathon, 21,000. Throughout his journey, he kept feeling better. He developed a liking for his job, which he had forcefully taken, and started getting better at it. With his performance at work improving, his income increased and he was less worried about supporting his family. He paved a career path for himself and even joined a few distance learning courses which he could manage alongside his job. Gradually, he found a love interest at his workplace too. His life was finally in his control, and he was in a happy place, both professionally and personally. Thus, exercising not only healed him, but also gave a good direction to his life.

Really, even starting out with five minutes of stretching at any time of the day can leave you feeling better. So, start building some time into your routine for this from now. Gradually keep increasing it a little and see how quickly the changes follow!

The Benefits of Exercising

- **Boosts your mood:** Exercise triggers the release of endorphins, often referred to as 'feel-good' hormones, which can help alleviate feelings of depression and anxiety, leading to an overall improvement in mood.
- **Increases your energy:** Regular physical activity enhances cardiovascular health, improving the efficiency of your heart and lungs. This leads to

increased stamina and energy levels, making daily tasks easier to perform.

- **Increases your productivity:** Exercise improves blood flow to the brain, which can enhance cognitive functions like memory and concentration. This can lead to better focus and productivity in both personal and professional tasks.
- **Makes you agile:** Engaging in activities that require coordination and flexibility, such as yoga or Pilates, can improve your agility, making you nimbler and less prone to injuries.
- **Makes you look good:** Regular exercise helps in maintaining a healthy weight and muscle tone, which can improve your physical appearance and boost your self-esteem.
- **Improves your skin health:** Exercise increases blood circulation, which helps deliver oxygen and nutrients to the skin. This can result in a healthier, more radiant complexion.
- **Protects your heart:** Cardiovascular exercises like running, swimming, or cycling strengthen the heart muscle, improve circulation, and help manage blood pressure and cholesterol levels, reducing the risk of heart disease.
- **Strengthens your joints:** Regular movement and weight-bearing exercises help keep joints flexible and strengthen the muscles around them, reducing the risk of joint pain and conditions like arthritis.

- **Strengthens your bones:** Weight-bearing exercises, such as walking, running, or lifting weights, stimulate bone formation and help prevent bone degeneration, reducing the risk of osteoporosis.
- **Reduces stress:** Physical activity can help lower the level of stress hormones, such as adrenaline and cortisol. It also stimulates the production of endorphins, which act as natural painkillers and mood elevators.
- **Lowers the risk of injury:** By improving strength, flexibility, and balance, regular exercise can help prevent injuries. Stronger muscles and better coordination reduce the likelihood of falls and other accidents.
- **Improves posture:** Strengthening the core muscles through exercises like planks and Pilates can improve posture, reducing the risk of back pain and other posture-related issues.
- **Improves creativity:** Exercise can boost creativity by increasing blood flow to the brain and reducing mental fatigue. Many people, including me, find that they have their best ideas while walking, running, or engaging in other forms of physical activity.
- **Improves fertility:** Regular exercise helps maintain a healthy weight and balance hormones, which can improve fertility in both men and women. It also reduces stress, which can have a positive impact on reproductive health.

- **Gives you confidence:** Achieving fitness goals and seeing improvements in your physical health can boost self-esteem and confidence. Feeling stronger and more capable can positively impact all areas of your life.

Now, if you still find it difficult to get yourselves going, then the following tips and tricks might be helpful

- Start small—maybe just five minutes a day.
- Don't make weight loss your focus.
- Try different types of exercises, like running, jogging, skipping, treadmill.
- Enjoy the type of workout you choose.
- Listening to some music while working out will keep you upbeat and focused.
- Don't lose heart if you have to skip a day or few days, but make it a point to get back.
- Manage time—exercise while doing laundry or watching TV. Be creative with your time.
- Have achievable goals. Don't be over ambitious, take it slow.
- Have reminders for yourself.

Resources

1. Read *Spark: The Revolutionary New Science of Exercise and the Brain* by John Ratey.

Food for Thought

1. If you regularly play a sport, how do you feel on days when you are unable to play it?
2. If you're not regular at any sport, how do you feel after playing one casually on a holiday with friends or kids?
3. Have you noted any difference in your mood and body movements before and after any exercise or play?

THOUGHT BREAK

Eat. Sleep. Work. Repeat.

Yes, that repeat mode is on unless interrupted by a vacation!

However, repetition isn't about being boring or being stuck in a rut.

Repetition brings discipline.

It brings progress.

And it brings experience.

If you work out, you would repeat your sets a certain number of times to tone that muscle. It's the same with life and work.

You need to tone those work muscles. Keep repeating and progressing until you get the results. With each iteration, you refine your skills, adapt to new challenges, and inch closer to your goals.

Can you turn your setbacks into comebacks?

Life is full of ups and downs, twists and turns. Despite that, have you ever thought that your setbacks are actually set-ups for your comebacks?

It's all about perspective. How you view the world around you can either hold you back or propel you forward.

Yes, there will be negativity around no matter how positive you are. But, don't repel it. Acknowledge it first, and then take a positive perspective. Find the lesson, the opportunity, or the silver lining.

By doing so, you'll unleash the positivity from within you and turn what could have been a setback into a powerful comeback.

Remember, every obstacle is a chance to grow, learn, and rise above.

The Power of Staying Hydrated: A Habit for Holistic Health

IMAGINE waking up in the morning feeling groggy, with brain fog, and your energy level at an all-time low. You reach for your phone to check the time and realise you have a full day ahead. What if I told you that a simple habit could transform your day, making you feel more energised, focused, and emotionally balanced? That habit is staying hydrated.

The Physical Benefits of Hydration

Water is the essence of life. Every cell, tissue, and organ in our body needs water to function correctly. Staying hydrated helps to maintain the balance of bodily fluids, which is crucial for digestion, circulation, and temperature regulation. When you're well-hydrated, your muscles work better, and you can push through physical activities with greater ease. Imagine running a marathon without water—it's nearly impossible!

The Mental Benefits of Hydration

But hydration isn't just about physical health; it plays a significant role in our cognitive functions. Have you ever felt sluggish or had difficulty concentrating? Dehydration might be the culprit. Studies have shown that even mild dehydration can impair cognitive performance, affecting memory, attention, and reaction time. By drinking enough water, you can keep your brain sharp and your mind clear.

The Emotional Benefits of Hydration

Our emotional well-being is also closely linked to our hydration levels. Dehydration can lead to mood swings, irritability, and increased stress levels. On the flip side, staying hydrated helps regulate mood and reduce anxiety. Think of hydration as a natural mood stabiliser that helps you feel balanced and emotionally resilient.

A Case Study by a Health Professional

Dr Emily, a renowned nutritionist, shares a compelling case study from her practice. She recalls a patient named John, a busy executive who struggled with chronic fatigue, headaches, and mood swings. Despite various treatments, his symptoms persisted. The doctor suggested a simple change: increase water intake. Within weeks, John noticed significant improvements. His headaches diminished, his energy levels soared, and his mood stabilised. This transformation highlights the profound impact of hydration on overall health.

Practical Tips for Staying Hydrated

Incorporating the habit of staying hydrated into your daily routine doesn't have to be complicated. Here are some practical tips:

- **Carry a Water Bottle:** Keep a reusable water bottle with you at all times. It serves as a constant reminder to drink water.
- **Set Reminders:** Use your phone or a hydration app to set regular reminders to drink water throughout the day.
- **Infuse Your Water:** If plain water feels boring, add a slice of lemon, cucumber, or mint for a refreshing twist.
- **Monitor Your Intake:** Aim for at least eight glasses of water a day, but remember that individual needs may vary.

Staying hydrated is a simple yet powerful habit that can transform your life. By making a conscious effort to drink more water, you can enhance your physical health, sharpen your mind, and stabilise your emotions. So, grab that water bottle, take a sip, and embrace the incredible benefits of staying hydrated. Your body, mind, and soul will thank you.

Start today by setting a hydration goal and tracking your progress. You'll be amazed at how this small habit can lead to big improvements in your overall well-being.

Food for Thought

1. How many glasses of water do you consume every day?
2. How do you feel on a winter day when you go without water for a long time?
3. How does your body feel when you consciously increase your water intake?

Gratitude and Thankfulness

We have already discussed the benefits of gratitude briefly under 'Journaling'. However, this habit in itself is so powerful that it deserves an entire chapter (or maybe a whole book). Let's explore gratitude and understand it from scratch.

What do we understand by gratitude?

The quality of being thankful, readiness to show appreciation, and to return kindness. Now, how can a simple act of thankfulness have an impact on all other spheres of life? Today, we are living in an era of knowledge and awareness. Profound research by mental health professionals on the impact of gratitude on the human brain found that gratitude writing can be beneficial not just for healthy, well-adjusted individuals but also for those who struggle with mental health concerns like depression, anxiety, and likewise. Gratitude is filled with the power to increase important neurochemicals because the thought process shifts from negative to positive. It helps in the release of the feel-good chemicals such as dopamine, serotonin, and oxytocin. Research also shows that there are about 1,200 chemical reactions that happen in the body when you're in a state of gratitude. Hence, they give rise to feelings of closeness, connection, and happiness.

While reading about right brain learning activities for my toddler, I discovered that gratitude was one of its foundational principles. It stressed the importance of practising it daily with your child before starting any kind of education. Finding time for being thankful for every little thing we have makes us humbler. The art of yoga also incorporates gratitude—Savasana requires being thankful for each and every part of the body. Even the smallest toe.

Pause before you complain. Think of the gifts you have.

Most of us must have either read or heard about the story of a blind boy with the signboard saying, 'I am blind, please help'. Passers-by would drop coins in his hat from time to time. One day, a man came, took the signboard, scribbled something on it, and kept it back. The blind boy then heard the hat rapidly filling up with coins. Many more people started giving him money.

A few days later, the man who had changed the sign came back and the blind boy recognised him by his footsteps. He asked him what he had written on the signboard. To this, the man responded, 'I only wrote the truth. I reiterated the same thing, but in a slightly different way. I wrote: "Today is a beautiful day, but I cannot see it".' While both the signs conveyed the same meaning, the second one just reminded people how grateful they should be for the ability to see. An impactful story.

* * *

Samaira was leading a happy life with her husband Nishant and their two children. The younger one had just turned one that year when Nishant had a paralysis attack and the left side of his body was left paralysed. He lost his job, and she quit hers to take care of him. They didn't have any source of income, and their medical expenses piled every day. Their medical insurance also lapsed with no premium payments that year. As if this was not enough, came another blow—Samaira lost her parents. She had no energy left in her to take care of the kids and Nishant. She felt hopeless and helpless. With no financial independence, no work, and a staggering stamina to even cook daily meals, she looked for online counselling. She needed help to fight the vortex of depression she was being pulled into and get her the strength to take care of her family.

The counsellor asked her to write a 'thank you' note each morning, expressing gratitude for one thing in her life. She felt agitated at this advice. What did she have to be thankful for? Zero income, rising debts, piling up medical expenses, deteriorating health, the guilt of being unable to give children a proper childhood? 'What do you think I should be grateful for?' she blurted out over the phone. Her counsellor responded calmly, 'Grateful for the roof over your head, which you own and don't rent.'

Something really shifted inside Samaira after this conversation, and she experienced a paradigm shift. She slept on this thought. The next morning, when she awoke, she retrieved a piece of paper and started writing, 'I am grateful for the air I am breathing. I am grateful for having a loving family and lovely kids.' After that day, she added more to that list of gratefulness every morning. She now had a newfound energy to take care of her husband, giving him physiotherapy lessons and taking him to the hospital for electrical stimulations. She took care of the kids with a smile on her face and patiently answered all of their curious questions. As a result, they felt more secure and loved, creating a pleasant atmosphere at home. There were major improvements in Nishant's condition within a few months, and he was able to move around. She took up a part-time job wherein she could work flexibly from her home, thus stabilising the finances to some extent. She was so fascinated by the idea of gratitude that she took to blogging to spread her positive thoughts and the impact of gratitude. In a year's time, Nishant fully recovered and his company re-hired him. Samaira couldn't have been more thankful and continued to express her gratitude for the tiniest of things in her life to the great blessings she got.

How Does Gratitude Work Its Magic?

What We Put Our Attention On Grows

It's the law of attraction at work here. Living in a state of negativity and lack makes us gravitate towards it subconsciously. When we shift our focus to abundance and all the good things in life, we get more of those.

Being Grateful Makes You Happy

Gratitude releases the feel-good hormones and makes you feel happy from within.

Improves Physical Health

Research shows that patients who practise gratitude experience less physical pains and tend to exercise more, taking care of their health.

Improves Emotional Health

It reduces the feelings of stress, anxiety, and depression. People practising gratitude possess greater control on their emotions, have reduced levels of cortisol, the stress hormone, and are better equipped to face any setbacks or negative experiences.

Helps in Getting Better Sleep

A simple act of thanksgiving activates our hypothalamus, the part of the brain that regulates all bodily mechanisms, sleep being one of them. Hence, someone who gets a deep, undisturbed sleep wakes up feeling refreshed and energetic.

Helps in Reducing Aggression

Grateful people are less likely to retaliate against others despite facing negative remarks. They are humble and rarely display harmful feelings towards anybody.

Improves Self-esteem

Grateful people don't harbour feelings of insecurity. They are more appreciative of other people's accomplishments and have no comparing attitude.

Improves Inter-Personal Relationships

The habit of saying 'thank you' more often not only helps win more friends but it also cultivates deeper, long-lasting, and harmonious relationships.

Helps You Reach Your Goals

Gratitude puts you in an inner state of personal victory, infusing happiness in your mind, body and soul. A happy mind works with a greater zeal towards its goals without getting distracted.

The list of the benefits can go on, but it's important to remember here that every change takes time. Besides, it also takes continuous reminders and practice to bring about this change. One needs to persevere and have faith. Slowly and steadily, all the good changes will come by.

How to practise gratitude?

- Write it down. This act makes it real and more connected to you. The best way to go about it is to keep a gratitude journal and write in it every day at a convenient time.
- Maintain your friendships. Truly value your friends. Share your gratitude with them.
- Spend more quality time with family and your loved ones.
- Give compliments frequently.
- See the silver lining everywhere. Whenever a negative thought comes to mind, or when you deal with adversity, change the lens and see the positivity in the situation.
- Reward efforts.
- Live in the present without regretting about the past or worrying about the future.
- Create visual reminders. Make a gratitude collage with pictures of people and things you are grateful for.

- Practise gratitude meditation.
- Volunteer and give back to society. Help others in the local community often.

Resource

1. Read *A Simple Act of Gratitude* by John Kralik.

Food for Thought

1. What do you feel when someone thanks you for a simple act like offering a glass of water? Would you want to pass that feeling on and thank others for their simple acts?
2. Will you try to consciously practise gratitude for the next seven days if you were told that this'll change your life and you'll get whatever you truly desire?
3. When was the last time you thanked someone? Do you remember when someone thanked you for something last?

THOUGHT BREAK

The Power of Silence: Unlocking a Profound and Better Self

In today's fast-paced world, chaos is inevitable. But what if I told you there's a way to rise above the noise and unlock a more profound and better version of yourself?

It starts with silence

Taking a few moments each day to experience silence can be transformative. As you practise being quiet and still, you'll begin to:

- Plan for the future with clarity and confidence, without anxiety
- Reflect on the past without regrets or dwelling
- Inhabit the present more fully, with focus and intention

Silence has the power to calm the mind, awaken creativity, and connect us with our inner selves

So, take a break from the chaos and tap into the power of silence. Your mind, body, and soul will thank you.

All is Well

There comes a time when we lose all hope

There comes a time when our vision is blurred

There comes a time when our plans don't work

That's the time of faith

That's the time of belief

Belief–in the bigger plan laid out for us which is definitely going to work

Belief–in a power that's beyond everything

All is well!

Plan Your Day in Advance

MEET Jane, a successful entrepreneur who runs a thriving technology start-up. Jane's days used to be chaotic, filled with back-to-back meetings, urgent emails, and constant firefighting. She often felt overwhelmed and struggled to find time for strategic thinking.

One day, Jane decided to try something new. Every evening, she spent just five minutes planning her next day. She listed her top priorities, scheduled her meetings, and set aside time for focused work. The results were astonishing. Jane found herself more organised and productive, and significantly less stressed. Her start-up flourished, as she could now dedicate quality time to innovation and growth.

From Jane's story, we learn the importance of prioritising tasks and setting aside time for focused work. By planning her day in advance, Jane could allocate her energy to what truly mattered, driving her business forward.

Lesson: Prioritise and Focus

Now, let's look at Mark, a busy parent juggling a demanding job and family responsibilities. Mark's mornings used to be a whirlwind of getting the kids ready for school, preparing breakfast, and rushing to work. He often felt exhausted before his workday even began.

Inspired by a friend, Mark started planning his next day the night before. He prepared the kids' lunches in advance, laid out their clothes, and even set the breakfast table. At work, he mapped out his tasks and scheduled breaks to recharge. This simple habit brought a sense of calm and control to his life. He felt more present with his family, and his productivity at work spiked.

Mark's experience teaches us the value of balancing personal and professional life through efficient planning. By organising his day in advance, he could better manage his time and energy, leading to a more harmonious life.

Lesson: Balance and Efficiency

Finally, consider Sarah, a college student with a packed schedule of classes, assignments, and extracurricular activities. Sarah often found herself procrastinating and cramming for exams at the last minute, leading to stress and subpar grades.

Determined to change, she adopted the habit of planning her day every evening. She created a study schedule, set specific goals for each day, and included time for relaxation and hobbies. This approach transformed her academic life. She became more disciplined, her grades improved, and she felt more in control of her time. Sarah's story highlights the role of planning in fostering discipline and personal growth. By setting clear goals and managing her time effectively, she achieved academic success and enjoyed a balanced life.

Lesson: Discipline and Growth

Tips for Planning Your Day

Here are some actionable tips to help you incorporate this habit into your daily routine:

- **Set a Specific Time:** Choose a consistent time each day to plan, such as before going to bed or the first thing in the morning.
- **Use a Planner or App:** Utilise tools like planners, calendars, or productivity apps to organise your tasks.
- **Prioritise Tasks:** Categorise tasks based on urgency and importance.
- **Be Realistic:** Set achievable goals and avoid overloading your schedule.
- **Review and Adjust:** At the end of the day, review your progress and adjust your plan for the next day if needed.

Common Challenges and Solutions

Some practical solutions for people who struggle with planning their day for various reasons:

- **Procrastination:** Break tasks into smaller, manageable chunks to make them less daunting.
- **Unexpected Interruptions:** Allocate buffer time in your schedule to accommodate unforeseen events.
- **Feeling Overwhelmed:** Focus on one task at a time and avoid multitasking.

The Transformative Outcome

Consistently planning your day in advance can lead to transformative outcomes. You'll find yourself more organised, less stressed, and better equipped to handle daily challenges. Over time, this habit can contribute to significant personal and professional growth.

In just five minutes, you can take control of your time and set yourself up for success. The habit of planning your day in advance is simple yet powerful. By incorporating this practice into your routine, you can unlock your full potential and lead a more fulfilling life.

Start today! Take five minutes to plan your tomorrow and witness the transformation.

It's true that not everything might go as planned. However, planning helps relieve some unnecessary stress, even preparing us for unforeseen and unexpected disruptions. The probability of achieving what you write down and plan are way higher than what you don't plan for.

Food for Thought

1. Have you tried working without making a task list and after making one? Which approach worked better for you?
2. If you could plan each aspect of your day and put it on paper, how would that look?
3. Does not having a plan to work with make you anxious and stressed?

Cultivate Mental Strength

FIRSTLY, what do we understand by this term 'mental toughness'?

According to Wikipedia, 'Mental toughness is a measure of individual resilience and confidence that may predict success in sport, education and the workplace.' It's often referred to as 'grit' as well. A proven fact from various research is that intelligence accounts for only 30% of success, and it is more about grit. Simply put, mental toughness is the degree of passion, perseverance, and determination one has to achieve their goals. Mentally tough people have a strong sense of purpose and are in better control of their lives.

This term can mean different things for different people. For a sportsperson, it might mean not missing a workout and sticking to a strict diet schedule; for a leader it might be about achieving a set target with the team on a daily basis; for a writer it might be writing at least 1000 words daily.

Let's explore the powerful story of Chris Gardner, a man who exemplified mental toughness in the face of overwhelming adversity.

Chris Gardner's Story: A Testament to Mental Toughness

Chris Gardner's journey is nothing short of extraordinary. In the early 1980s, Gardner found himself struggling to make ends meet. He was a salesman with a dream to make it big, but life had other plans. Faced with homelessness, a failed relationship, and the responsibility of raising his young son, his situation seemed hopeless. Yet, he refused to give up.

Gardner's turning point came when he saw a man stepping out of a red Ferrari. Intrigued, he asked the man what he did for a living. The answer? He was a stockbroker. This encounter ignited a spark in Gardner. Despite having no experience or connections, he set his sights on becoming a stockbroker.

Gardner's path was fraught with obstacles. He juggled multiple jobs, slept in shelters, and even spent nights in public restrooms with his son. But his perseverance never wavered. He secured an unpaid internship at a prestigious brokerage firm, working tirelessly to prove himself. His resilience, positive thinking, and ability to manage stress were his greatest allies.

After months of relentless effort, his hard work paid off. He not only completed the internship but also landed a full-time position. His story, immortalised in the film, *The Pursuit of Happyness*, is a powerful reminder that mental toughness can turn even the direst of situations into opportunities for growth.

From this anecdote, we can extract these valuable lessons on mental toughness:

- **Perseverance:** Gardner's unwavering determination kept him moving forward, even when the odds were stacked against him. This teaches us that perseverance is about consistently pursuing our goals, regardless of setbacks.
- **Resilience:** Life's challenges are inevitable, but resilience allows us to bounce back stronger. Gardner's ability to recover from failures and keep striving is a testament to the power of resilience.
- **Positive Thinking:** Gardner maintained a positive outlook, focusing on his goals rather than his hardships. Positive thinking helps us see opportunities where others see obstacles.
- **Stress Management:** Gardner's ability to manage stress was crucial. He balanced the pressures of his internship, fatherhood, and homelessness with remarkable composure. Effective stress management techniques, such as mindfulness and time management, are essential for maintaining mental toughness.

Now, how to build mental toughness? It's about going that extra mile when you are just on the verge of giving up. It's about the small wins. It's about lifting that weight for the twentieth rep when you were about to stop at seventeen. It's about writing that extra page when you were about to wrap up at just two for the day. Regularly increasing these small wins, hence, leads to a stronger and mentally tougher 'you'. How? Take a pause anytime you catch yourself blaming others, taking everything so seriously, or giving in to distraction. Stop blaming the past or external factors for the choices you make.

The following steps can help achieve this mental toughness:

- **Emotional Stability:** Leaders need to take most of the important decisions under stressful and pressurised circumstances. Hence, emotional stability is important in those overwhelming scenarios to have clarity of the circumstances.
- **Strength under stress:** Maintain calm, composure, and resilience when negative pressures try to bog you down. Incorporate practices like meditation, exercise, and time management into your routine to handle stress effectively.
- **Detachment:** Try not to take any negative comments personally. Rather, focus on what can be controlled.
- **Positive Self-talk:** Yes, positive affirmations also help in building resilience and mental toughness. Replace negative thoughts with them. Focus on what you can control and maintain an optimistic outlook.
- **Control:** It's necessary to discern what comes under your circle of influence and concern and what doesn't—that is, things and circumstances you can control or influence, and circumstances beyond your control. Once this is figured out, it is easier to

control our actions and emotions and not give away the power to others to control us and our reactions.

- **Tenacity:** As explained in the examples above, never give up. Keep pushing forward, even when progress seems slow. Remember, perseverance is the key to achieving long-term success.

A sentence most suitable here is, 'Mental toughness is about your habits, not your motivation.'

To conclude, Chris Gardner's story is a powerful example of how mental toughness can transform your life. By embracing perseverance, resilience and determination, one can combat the hardest of challenges and achieve what they truly desire. Appearing for my final professional exams for Chartered Accountancy was also one such journey where my mental toughness was tested—when I couldn't clear the exams in my first two attempts. It was depressing and made me miserable, but unwavering perseverance and resilience helped me get through it.

Food for Thought

1. Recall a time when your endurance was truly tested but you finally reached the outcome—maybe in a gym training session or a professional project.
2. Where would you set your mental limits if you knew it was in your hands and your mental limits would decide the outcome?

THOUGHT BREAK

Don't Let Vacations Interrupt Your Passions

Have you ever judged someone for sticking to their routine, like going to the gym, while on vacation? I know I have. But, here's the thing: when something becomes a passion, it's no longer a chore.

I used to think waking up early on a holiday was crazy, until I realised my body clock had become automatic. Certain routines and passions become ingrained in us, and we can't break free from them—nor do we want to.

That's the power of passion. It flows out of us, irrespective of time and place. Whether you're on vacation or not, your passion will drive you to pursue it.

So, don't let vacations interrupt your passions.

Instead, find ways to incorporate them into your travels. You never know what new experiences and opportunities might arise.

Remember, passions make life worth living. They bring us joy, fulfilment, and a sense of purpose.

Four reminders to power you through your day!

- Difficult days also pass
- Your vision is greater than your difficulties
- A tiny step made in the right direction is also progress
- Keep going no matter what comes your way

Had it been easy, you wouldn't have been YOU.

Certain things are meant to be HARD.

Otherwise, they're not valued.

You enjoy the sweetness of honey?

Well, it's loaded with the hard work of bees and the person who risks the bee stings to procure it and get it to you in a bottle.

You want to taste success.

Well, if it's a valued place to reach, then you got to take the bullshit at times and not complain about it.

Had it been a cakewalk, everyone would've taken it, making it less valuable.

What you BECOME in the process is more important than what you achieve.

In tough times, just remember it's meant to BE tough, for you to BECOME tougher!

Curiosity Doesn't Kill the Cat

IMAGINE a world where curiosity is the driving force behind every action, where the habit of asking questions opens doors to personal development, professional growth, educational success, and exceptional leadership. This chapter explores the transformative power of asking questions, drawing inspiration from real-life examples, including the remarkable journey of Dr APJ Abdul Kalam.

Unlocking Personal Development

Asking questions is a cornerstone of personal growth. It pushes us beyond our comfort zones, encouraging us to explore new ideas and perspectives. When we ask questions, we challenge our assumptions and broaden our understanding.

Consider the story of Steve Jobs, co-founder of Apple Inc. Jobs was known for his relentless questioning, which drove innovation and creativity within his team. His habit of asking 'Why?' and 'What if?' led to ground-breaking products like the iPhone and iPad. By cultivating a habit of questioning, we too can ignite our curiosity and unlock our potential.

Fuelling Professional Growth

In the professional world, asking questions is a powerful tool for growth and success. It demonstrates engagement, fosters collaboration, and drives continuous improvement.

Take the example of Sara Blakely, the founder of Spanx. Blakely's journey began with a simple question: 'Why isn't there a better alternative to traditional pantyhose?' This question sparked her entrepreneurial spirit and led to the creation of a billion-dollar empire. By asking questions, professionals can identify opportunities, solve problems, and drive innovation.

Achieving Educational Success

In educational settings, the habit of asking questions is essential for deep learning and intellectual growth. It encourages critical thinking, enhances comprehension, and fosters a love for learning.

Consider the story of Malala Yousafzai, the youngest Nobel Prize laureate. Malala's habit of questioning societal norms and advocating for female education has inspired millions worldwide. Her questions challenged the status quo and brought about significant change. In classrooms, students who ask questions are more likely to engage with the material, understand complex concepts, and excel academically.

Enhancing Leadership Skills

Effective leaders are often characterised by their ability to ask insightful questions. This habit enables them to understand their teams, identify challenges, and make informed decisions.

Jeff Bezos, the founder of Amazon, exemplifies this trait. Bezos's leadership style involves asking questions that encourage his team to think critically and explore new possibilities. His famous question, 'What's not going to change in the next ten years?' has guided Amazon's long-term strategy and success. By asking questions, leaders can inspire their teams, nurture innovation, and drive organisational growth.

The Inspirational Journey of APJ Abdul Kalam

Dr APJ Abdul Kalam, the former President of India and a renowned scientist, is a shining example of the transformative power of asking questions. Born into a humble family, Kalam's insatiable curiosity and habit of questioning fuelled his journey from a small town in Tamil Nadu to the highest office in India.

His early life was marked by his quest for knowledge. As a student, he constantly asked questions, seeking to understand the world around him. This habit continued throughout his career, leading to significant contributions in India's space and missile programs. His question, 'How can India become self-reliant in technology?' drove his efforts to advance the nation's scientific capabilities.

Kalam's leadership and vision were deeply rooted in this habit of asking questions. He believed that questioning was essential for innovation and progress. His famous quote, 'Dream, dream, dream. Dreams transform into thoughts and thoughts result in action' reflects his belief in the power of curiosity and inquiry.

Embrace the Habit of Asking Questions

In every sphere of life, the habit of asking questions can be a catalyst for growth and success. Whether it's personal development, professional growth, educational achievement, or leadership excellence, asking questions empowers us to explore new possibilities, challenge the status quo, and drive meaningful change.

So, let us embrace this habit with enthusiasm and curiosity. Let us ask questions that inspire, challenge, and transform.

See the world through a child's lens. Asking questions about everything is the way a child learns about the world. As we grow up, we start taking things for granted and don't bother to get into the logical aspect of it. Asking questions to ourselves and to others helps us grow and get a different perspective, enabling us to think out of the box and come up with creative ideas and solutions.

Call to Action

Spend a day with any three-year old and you'll understand the joy of curiosity and questioning every logic until you're satisfied. My four-year old daughter's favourite question to trouble me with is—how did God make people? What did he use to make the eyes, hair, nails, and skin? My life will become easier if AI tells me the ingredients and the processes of all these!

Food for Thought

1. Do you consider yourself a curious person? If no, think about what holds you back from being curious.
2. Have you ever been scolded or judged for asking 'too many' questions? If yes, how did you feel? What did you learn?

Learn a New Skill Regularly

As soon as the final results of my Chartered Accountancy exams were declared, I was relieved to know that I had cleared it. To my naïve mind, it meant I didn't need to study anymore. What I didn't realise was that the real-life lessons and teachings had just begun.

Life really does have its own way to teach us, and if we don't have a student mind-set—filled with the curiosity to understand and question everything—we are not going to get far. If we don't learn, adapt, and change with the times, then our tools (skills) are sure to get rusty and dated. We won't be relevant anymore.

Be it a job, a sport, or any skill that either puts bread and butter on your table or fuels your heart and soul, you need to sharpen the saw. We are living at a time when we have an ocean of resources and knowledge in our hands—on our very phones. Thus, it's all about taking action and tapping into the power of knowledge.

In a rapidly changing world, the ability to learn and adapt is more valuable than ever. Regularly acquiring new skills not only keeps you relevant but also enriches your personal and professional life.

The Power of Continuous Learning

Learning new skills is akin to adding tools to a toolbox. Each skill equips you to handle different challenges and seize opportunities. Whether it's mastering a new language, picking up a musical instrument, or understanding the basics of coding, every new skill opens up a world of possibilities.

Real Life Stories

A school in Punjab, known as Bebe-Bapu (mother-father), teaches the elderly to read and write. Those who were not privileged enough to go to school in their childhood come here to learn these skills. They feel proud when they are able to sign for themselves on any documents instead of putting their thumb impressions. They feel empowered when they are able to read the signboards without asking anyone what's written on them.

Learning is not limited to basic and professional education. It goes much beyond.

Harsh Mariwala, the Chairman of Marico Limited, exemplifies continuous learning in corporate India. Starting with his family's trading business, he transformed it into a leading consumer goods company by relentlessly pursuing knowledge about branding, marketing, and consumer behaviour. Without formal business education, Harsh sought insights from industry experts, books, and best global practices, attending workshops and seminars to stay ahead. His dedication to learning and innovation led to the success of brands like Parachute and Saffola, fostering a culture of continuous improvement within Marico. His ongoing commitment to staying updated about industry trends and mentoring young entrepreneurs underscores the transformative power of lifelong learning in driving corporate success.

This really shows that there is no age for learning, and learning itself is infinite.

Types of Skills You Can Learn

- **Technical Skills:** These include coding, data analysis, and digital marketing. In today's tech-driven world, technical skills are crucial for career advancement.
- **Soft Skills:** Communication, teamwork, and leadership are essential for personal and professional relationships. Developing these skills can lead to more effective collaboration and conflict resolution.
- **Creative Skills:** Artistic pursuits like painting, writing, and music not only provide a creative outlet but also enhance cognitive abilities and emotional well-being.
- **Life Skills:** These include time management, financial literacy, and critical thinking. Life skills are fundamental for navigating everyday challenges and making informed decisions.
- **Sports Skills:** Engaging in sports improves physical health, teaches discipline, and fosters a sense of teamwork and perseverance.

Also, whatever skills and expertise you have, make a habit to pass it on and teach it to someone who needs or wants it. This not only makes you a teacher but also improves your skills. The best way to learn anything is by teaching it.

The ever-changing economic scenario has given rise to boundless creative professions like influencer marketing, personal branding, image specialist, online teaching and what not. It's never too late to research and upskill yourself.

Challenges and Solutions

For Students

Balancing academic responsibilities with learning new skills can be daunting. However, integrating skill development into daily routines, such as setting aside time for online courses or joining clubs, can make it manageable. Pursuing a professional course or attending college in a new city away from the comfort of home itself comes with a plethora of challenges. Equipping yourself with certain life skills is a game changer, like managing finances on a limited budget, allotting time for household chores, besides attending classes and studying.

For Professionals

A fast-paced work environment often leaves little time for skill acquisition. Prioritising learning by scheduling it into your calendar and leveraging resources like webinars and workshops can help. Your existing technical knowledge can help you land a job, but you need to hone those skills to thrive in it. Working on soft skills, networking, and managing teams is something that can land you a platinum project at work and pave a stronger career path.

For the General Public

Finding motivation and resources can be challenging. Setting clear goals, seeking out community classes, or using online platforms like Coursera and Udemy can provide structure and support.

The habit of learning new skills regularly is a powerful tool for growth and success. Whether you're a student, a professional, or simply someone eager to expand your horizons, embracing this habit can lead to a richer, more fulfilling life. So, what new skill will you learn today?

Resource

1. Read *The Final Diagnosis* by Arthur Hailey.

Food for Thought

1. What was the last skill that you had invested time and resources for to learn and develop?
2. Would you invest in learning new skills if it was the only thing that would help you stay relevant and up to date in the long run?

THOUGHT BREAK

Do you ask yourself this when you end your day?

As I reflect on my day, I realise that a single question can make all the difference. If I could ask myself one question every day before sleeping, it would be,

'Did I live today better than yesterday?'

This simple question prompts me to reflect on my actions, decisions, and experiences. It encourages me to:

- Celebrate my wins, no matter how small
- Learn from my mistakes and setbacks
- Identify areas for improvement
- Set intentions for a better tomorrow

A day is our life in miniature. How we live our days is how we live our lives. By asking myself this question daily, I'm reminded to:

- Make the most of every moment
- Be present and mindful
- Embrace challenges and opportunities
- Grow and learn continuously

Let's strive to live each day better than the last, and in doing so, create a life that truly reflects our values, aspirations, and dreams.

Do you often doubt your skills, successes, and self-worth?

You're not alone. Imposter syndrome is common, but it doesn't have to hold you back.

Here are some practical daily actions to help you overcome it:

- Replace 'I'm fake' with 'I'm capable and competent'
- Celebrate your achievements and skills
- Ask trusted colleagues or mentors for feedback to build confidence
- Take care of your physical and mental well-being
- View failures as opportunities for growth and learning
- Build a supportive network of colleagues and friends
- Develop new skills and expand your knowledge

Remember, imposter syndrome is not a reflection of your abilities but a common experience many professionals face.

By taking these daily actions, you can build confidence, overcome self-doubt, and reach your full potential.

The Art of Listening

THE art of listening is immensely powerful and comes with its own set of benefits. By actively and empathetically listening, one can understand the other person's perspective better. It enhances one's relationships. It even helps us become better leaders. However, the skill of listening is quite an understated one. Listening is as important as communicating (in fact, the process of communication includes listening. Without it, the process is incomplete). It's a required skill not only in your profession but even to maintain your personal relationships. Sometimes, we don't need any solutions. All we need is a listening ear. Be that ear for someone, and you'd mean the world to them in that moment.

It's important to distinguish between listening and hearing. While hearing is just an automatic brain response to any sound, listening in its best form is focused, voluntary, and intentional. I have often found myself daydreaming and struggling to actively listen if the topic is uninteresting or the speaker is not a good orator. This has often led me to lose out on valuable information. However, it's not just classroom listening that we should develop but also listening in all our day-to-day interactions. For building this habit, one needs to make conscious efforts and practise mindful listening. With this, one can build great interpersonal relations. It helps in becoming a better student; you build a perspective of your own and it further aids in public speaking.

* * *

In the bustling city of Bengaluru, there was a young professional named Priya. She worked at a technology company and was known for her multitasking abilities, often juggling multiple projects at once. One day, her manager, Mr Iyer, called for an important team meeting to discuss the upcoming client presentation. Priya, eager to stay on top of her tasks, brought her laptop and continued working on her code while her manager spoke. He detailed the client's specific requirements and the key points that needed to be highlighted in the presentation. Priya, half-listening, occasionally nodded and said, 'Yes, got it' while typing away furiously.

A few days later, it was her turn to present to the client. She confidently started her presentation, only to realise halfway that she missed several crucial points her manager had mentioned. The client looked unimpressed, and Mr Iyer's expression was a mix of frustration and disappointment.

After the meeting, Mr Iyer gently pulled Priya aside and told her, 'Priya, I know you're great at multitasking, but sometimes, it's important to focus on listening. It can make all the difference.'

Remove your headphones, step out of your heads,
and live in the present.

In corporate and leadership lessons, listening is one such trait that is now being emphasised, whether for employee satisfaction, client retention and acquiring new clients, or collaborations. None of these can be effectively achieved without active listening.

Benefits of Active Listening

Improved Understanding

Active listening helps you fully comprehend the message being conveyed, reducing misunderstandings and errors.

Better Relationships

It fosters trust and respect in both personal and professional relationships, as people feel valued and heard.

Enhanced Problem-Solving

By truly understanding the issues at hand, you can develop more effective solutions and make better decisions.

Increased Productivity

Clear communication leads to more efficient workflow and reduces the need to rework or clarify.

Greater Empathy

It allows you to see things from others' perspectives, fostering empathy and improving interpersonal dynamics.

Higher Retention

Active listening helps you remember information better, which is crucial in both learning environments and professional settings.

Imagine you're in a team meeting where a colleague is presenting a new project idea. Here's how you can practise active listening:

- **Maintain Eye Contact:** Look at your colleague while they speak.

- **Avoid Interrupting:** Let them finish their presentation without interjecting.
- **Show That You're Listening:** Nod and smile to show that you're engaged.
- **Provide Feedback:** After they finish, say, 'I understand that you're proposing a new marketing strategy that focuses on social media influencers. Is that correct?'
- **Ask Questions:** Follow up with, 'Can you explain how this strategy will differ from our current approach?'
- **Avoid Distractions:** Keep your phone on silent and focus on the discussion.
- **Be Patient:** Allow your colleague to answer fully before you respond.
- **Respond Appropriately:** Offer constructive feedback or support based on what you've heard.
- **Practise Empathy:** Acknowledge their effort by saying, 'I can see you've put a lot of thought into this. Thank you for your hard work.'
- **Take Notes:** Write down key points to refer back to later.

By incorporating these active listening techniques, you can enhance your communication skills, build stronger relationships, and improve overall effectiveness in both personal and professional settings.

Food for Thought

1. Have you struggled recalling what was discussed in a meeting if you were not actively listening?
2. Do you feel frustrated when you're asked to repeat something you've already clearly mentioned just because the other person wasn't attentively listening?

The Power of Kindness

ONE fine summer afternoon in June, as I was working from home and engrossed in work calls, I ordered lunch via Zomato. As the doorbell rang, I got up along with my laptop in one hand while still on a call. I opened the door and took the order from the delivery guy. As I was closing the door, I noticed that the guy tried to signal something to me but refrained after seeing me on call.

I realised that he wanted a glass of water. Without wasting another second, I pulled the door open, asked him to wait, excused myself from the call, and got him a glass of water. For me, it was just taking out a minute, but for him that glass of water meant a lot in that scorching summer heat. This incident taught me that even the smallest gestures of kindness take a minute but get you a lifetime of blessings.

Imagine a world where everyone lent a helping hand. Picture the smiles, the gratitude, and the sheer joy that would ripple through our communities. This chapter dives into the profound impact of helping others and how this simple habit can transform your mental and emotional well-being.

The Ripple Effect of Kindness

Helping others is like tossing a pebble into a pond. The initial splash may seem small, but the ripples extend far beyond the point of impact. When you help someone, you're not just making their day better; you're setting off a chain reaction of positivity. Acts of kindness inspire others to pay it forward, creating a community where support and compassion flourish.

Mental and Emotional Benefits

Increased Happiness

Helping others releases endorphins, the brain's natural feel-good chemicals. This phenomenon, often referred to as the 'helper's high', boosts your mood and overall happiness. Just think about the last time you did something kind for someone—didn't it make you feel amazing?

Improved Self-Esteem

When you help others, you reinforce your sense of self-worth. Knowing that you've made a positive impact on someone's life can significantly boost your confidence and self-esteem. It's a reminder that you have the power to change the world, one small act at a time.

Reduced Stress

Engaging in acts of kindness can lower your stress levels. Helping others takes your mind off your own worries and provides a sense of purpose and fulfilment. It's a natural stress reliever that benefits both the giver and the receiver.

Strengthened Social Connections

Helping others fosters a sense of community and belonging. It strengthens your social bonds and creates a support network that you can rely on. These connections are vital for mental and emotional health, providing comfort and encouragement during tough times.

Oprah Winfrey's Journey

Oprah Winfrey's life is a testament to the transformative power of helping others. From her humble beginnings to becoming a global icon, she has consistently used her platform to uplift others. Her philanthropic efforts, such as the Oprah Winfrey Leadership Academy for Girls in South Africa, have changed countless lives.

From her *Oprah's Favourite Things* episodes to her generous donations and educational causes, Oprah's acts of kindness have not only uplifted countless lives but also brought immense joy to her own.

Her commitment to helping others stems from her own experiences. She has often spoken about how acts of kindness from others helped her during difficult times. By paying it forward, she has created a legacy of compassion and generosity. Oprah's journey shows us that helping others is not just about giving; it's about creating opportunities for growth and empowerment.

Call to Action

Ready to make a difference? Here are some practical steps to incorporate the habit of helping others into your daily life:

- **Volunteer:** Find a local organisation that aligns with your passions and dedicate some time each week to volunteer.
- **Offer Support:** Be there for your friends and family. Sometimes, lending an ear or offering a helping hand can make all the difference.
- **Random Acts of Kindness:** Perform small acts of kindness, like buying coffee for a stranger or leaving a positive note for a co-worker.

Helping others is a powerful habit that can transform your life and of those around you. By making kindness a part of your daily routine, you will experience increased happiness, improved self-esteem, reduced stress, and stronger social connections. Take a page from Oprah Winfrey's life's book and start making a positive impact today. Remember, every act of kindness counts. Start your journey of helping others today and watch the ripples of positivity spread far and wide.

Food for Thought

1. Think about a random act of kindness shown to you. How did it make you feel?
2. Think about the instances when you were kind to others.

THOUGHT BREAK

When was the last time you did nothing?

No, really, nothing. No scrolling, no emailing, no multitasking. Just pure, unadulterated nothingness.

How did you feel after that?

Did you feel relaxed? Cleared your mind? Solved a problem you had been dealing with or struck an idea?

Building in some free time in our schedule is a great way to increase productivity.

In today's fast-paced world, we're always told to hustle, grind, and push ourselves to the extreme limit. But what if I told you that doing nothing can actually increase your productivity?

Building free time into our schedules allows us to:

- Recharge and reduce burnout

- Clear mental clutter and focus on what matters
- Tap into our creative subconscious and spark new ideas
- Approach problems with fresh eyes and innovative solutions

So, take a break from the hustle and bustle. Schedule some 'nothing' time into your day.

Your mind (and productivity) will thank you.

Broaden Your Horizons by Travelling

THE world is full of wonderful things you haven't seen yet. Don't ever give up on the chance of seeing them.
– JK Rowling

And you wonder, why a chapter on travel? How can travelling be a habit? Isn't it supposed to be a hobby?

Aamir Khan once said in an interview that one advice that he gives to new faces in the industry is, 'If you want to be an actor in Indian cinema, travel around the country alone with a bag pack!'

Well, yes, it is a hobby, but what if it can be a habit? Travelling isn't always supposed to be to an exotic destination with fancy tourist spots and scenic views. It can be a weekly travel to a place where you find peace and happiness, even if it is a short drive with your partner, child, or just yourself. A spot within the city where you can drop by when you feel like. The joy of driving, riding a bike, or just walking (if you are a long-distance walker and if it's safe for you) is incomparable. Travelling gives the luxury of indulging in yourself and slowing down, and you get the time to observe your surroundings.

Embrace the Habit of Travelling

Travelling, whether it's a short daily commute or an adventurous long-distance journey, holds the power to transform our lives in profound ways. It's not just about reaching a destination; it's about the experiences, learning, and personal growth that occur along the way.

The Benefits of Travelling

Travel is more than just a physical movement from one place to another. It's a journey of the soul and mind. When we travel, we step out of our comfort zones and open ourselves to new experiences. This habit can significantly enhance our lives by broadening our perspectives, fostering cultural understanding, and providing a much-needed break from our everyday routine.

Everyday Travel

Everyday travel, such as commuting to work or taking a walk in a different neighbourhood, might seem mundane, but it holds its own unique set of benefits. These daily movements can serve as mini-adventures, offering moments of reflection, relaxation, and even inspiration. A simple change in scenery can invigorate the mind and spark creativity. Imagine taking a different route to work and discovering a quaint coffee shop or a beautiful park you never knew existed. These small discoveries can add joy and excitement to our daily lives.

Long-Distance Travel

Long-distance travel takes us further away from home, but closer to the heart of adventure. It's about immersing ourselves in new cultures, tasting exotic foods, and witnessing breathtaking landscapes. The excitement of planning a trip, the thrill of the journey, and the memories created along the way are invaluable. It enriches our lives by teaching us about the world and, more importantly, about ourselves. It challenges our assumptions, broadens our horizons, and fosters a deeper appreciation for the diversity of life.

Lives of Travellers (Going Beyond Just Travel)

Throughout history, many travellers have left indelible marks on the world, inspiring generations to come. Let's get to know some in the current era:

- **Naveen Rabelli** is an engineer who travelled from India to the UK in a solar-powered tuk-tuk. His journey was not just an adventure but a mission to promote sustainable transportation and renewable energy. Naveen's travels have raised awareness about the importance of eco-friendly travel solutions and inspired many to consider alternative energy sources. His innovative approach to travel has had a lasting impact on the conversation around sustainability.

- **Ajeet Bajaj** is an adventurer and the first Indian to complete the Polar Trilogy, which includes skiing to the North Pole, South Pole, and across Greenland. His habit of travelling and exploring extreme environments has not only brought him personal fulfilment but also led to significant contributions in the field of adventure tourism in India. Ajeet runs Snow Leopard Adventures, an adventure travel company that promotes sustainable and responsible tourism. His journeys have inspired many to embrace adventure and conservation.

* * *

Travelling, in any form, is a habit that can profoundly impact our lives. It teaches us resilience, adaptability, and empathy. It helps us to grow, thrive, and see the world through a different lens. So, whether it's a short trip to a nearby town or an epic journey across continents, embrace the habit of travelling. Let it inspire, challenge, and enrich your life in ways you've never imagined.

Travel provides one with the best stories to share with friends, family, and children, full of adventurous treks, enjoyable road trips, or playful beachy stories. It is the best break you can give yourself from the monotony of daily life. It makes family bonds stronger, creates deeper friendships, and gives you endless memories and stories to share. Whether close to nature or on a busy road, a traveller's vision will always give you a fresh perspective.

Resources

1. Read *Eat, Pray, Love* by Elizabeth Gilbert.
2. Read *The Shooting Star: A Girl, Her Backpack and the World* by Shivya Nath.

Food for Thought

1. What has been your best travel experience so far? What made it the best—the destination, journey, the company, or something else?
2. How frequently do you want to travel in a year? How can you plan and make it work?

'Me' Time

JOHN Wood, the author of *Leaving Microsoft to Change the World*, is an inspiring example of how finding 'me time' can lead to profound personal and professional transformation. John was a high-powered executive at Microsoft, climbing the corporate ladder and achieving significant success. However, despite his professional accomplishments, he felt a lingering sense of dissatisfaction and burnout.

During a vacation to Nepal, John decided to take some much-needed 'me time'. This break from his hectic schedule allowed him to reflect on his life and priorities. It was during this trip that he visited a local school and was struck by the lack of resources and opportunities available to the children. This experience ignited a passion within him to make a difference.

John's decision to leave Microsoft and establish Room to Read, a non-profit organisation dedicated to improving literacy and gender equality in education, was a direct result of the clarity and inspiration he gained during his 'me time'. Today, Room to Read has impacted millions of children worldwide, and John credits his success to that pivotal moment of rest and reflection.

Just like John, this realisation for 'me time' came to me as well. In my case, I realised it after becoming a mother. Even though I had sufficient support at home to take care of the baby, I was constantly occupied—either physically or mentally, thinking about ordering medicines, clothes, nappies, vaccinations and what not.

Every minute of my waking hours was occupied with actions and thoughts to accomplish as much as possible. Be it my schedule at work or my household chores and parenting tasks. It was a circle; it just didn't end.

I realised that if 'me time' was not consciously built, then you wouldn't ever get it. You might complain and crib about it, but you are the one who needs to selfishly snatch it from the overwhelming tasks each day.

In today's fast-paced world, the importance of resting and finding 'me time' often gets overlooked. Yet, this habit is crucial for boosting mental health, improving productivity, achieving work-life balance, and fostering personal growth. Taking time to rest and recharge isn't a luxury, it's a necessity. Hence, everyone should be entitled to it. Even home-makers and housewives—responsible for the togetherness of the entire family and always on their toes to keep the home in order—need it. They cannot pour from an empty cup. 'Me time' gives you the space to take care of yourself and fill your cup. Fill it to the brim or even let it overflow without feeling any guilt.

The Benefits of Resting and Finding 'Me Time'

- **Mental Health:** Regular breaks reduce stress and anxiety, promoting a healthier mind.
- **Productivity:** Taking time to recharge can boost focus and efficiency, leading to better performance.
- **Work-Life Balance:** 'Me time' helps to maintain a healthy balance between professional responsibilities and personal interests.
- **Personal Growth:** Reflection and self-care foster personal development and a deeper understanding of oneself.

Resting and finding 'me time' are essential habits for anyone looking to improve their mental health, productivity, and overall quality of life. Whether you're a high-powered executive like John Wood, a new mother, or a homemaker, taking out time for yourself can lead to remarkable transformations.

Call to Action

Reflect on your current habits and consider how you can incorporate more rest and 'me time' into your daily routine. Start small and gradually increase the time you dedicate to self-care. Remember, investing in yourself is the first step towards achieving your full potential.

Take a moment today to schedule your 'me time' and experience the benefits first hand.

Food for Thought

1. What does 'me time' look like to you?
2. Do your loved ones devote time to themselves? If no, will you encourage them to do so henceforth?

THOUGHT BREAK

Did you have a stressful day?

'Every day brings a choice, to practice stress or to prepare peace.' – Joan Borysenko.

As corporate professionals, we often view stress as a nemesis, a hindrance to our well-being and productivity. However, what if I tell you that stress can be a valuable ally in short doses?

Think about it.

Stress-testing is a deliberate process used to assess the limits of a system, material or individual. It's a controlled exposure to stress that helps to identify strengths and weaknesses, allowing for improvements and growth.

You will also rely on a product if it has successfully gone through stress-testing procedures.

Similarly, in our professional lives, short-term stress can:

- Enhance focus and concentration
- Boost creativity and problem-solving skills
- Increase productivity and motivation
- Develop resilience and adaptability

The key is to recognise when stress is becoming counterproductive and take proactive steps to manage it. So, let's reframe our perspective on stress. Instead of viewing it as a constant enemy, let's harness its power to drive our success.

Embrace stress as a catalyst for growth, and remember that a little stress can go a long way in making you stronger, more agile, and resilient in the corporate world.

Music, the Silent Healer

AGAIN, would this be a hobby or a habit? Well, if done regularly then why not a habit?

In the hustle and bustle of modern life, finding moments of peace and solace can be challenging. Yet, one universal remedy that transcends cultures and generations is music. The habit of listening to music is not just a pastime but a powerful tool for enhancing mental health, emotional well-being, and stress relief. This chapter explores the profound impact of music on our health and delves into the inspiring life story of rapper, Divine, whose journey exemplifies the transformative power of music.

As toddlers, we are introduced to music in the form of nursery rhymes and lullabies—something that calms us when we are cranky and even makes us sleep. When I started early learning for my few-month-old daughter to develop her right brain and creative side, I came across activities which advocated the idea of introducing musical notes and beats to toddlers early on. Anything can be taught to children if it is in musical forms and hence, we have innumerable kids' rhymes, from teaching them about body parts and numbers to healthy eating habits.

We tend to forget this magic of music as we grow old. Research has shown that music is a therapy; it's a healer along with being a good entertainer and a teacher. Music can cure illness and depression. It reduces pain, stress, and anxiety and even improves the brain's memorising power. Music affects our emotions—listening to upbeat music lifts our mood while listening to a sad song makes us feel sad. Listening to energetic songs boosts our energy levels while listening to calm songs puts us in a calm state of mind.

Now, music comes in a variety of genres and everyone has different tastes. I would say that when trying to build music as a habit, follow your feeling and listen to what makes you feel good. The benefits will follow on their own. You may have separate playlists for different activities. For example, an upbeat one for exercising, running, or working out; a quirky one while you're cooking; a soothing, calm one while working on an important project at work, to help you concentrate. Goes without saying, you'd need a totally different one when you're partying and have your dancing shoes on.

Each type of music has its own set of benefits and varying levels of importance to different people as per their tastes and moods. When it comes to building a habit of listening to music, I would stress the importance of listening to alpha waves for a while every day to improve brain power and concentration. Again, this is a concept I came across while researching right brain education for my girl.

Health Benefits of Listening to Music

Listening to music is more than just a form of entertainment; it's a therapeutic practice with numerous health benefits.

Mental Health

Music has a unique ability to influence our brain chemistry. Listening to your favourite tunes can trigger the release of dopamine, the 'feel-good' neurotransmitter, which can help alleviate symptoms of depression and anxiety. For corporate professionals and students alike, integrating music into daily routines can provide a much-needed mental boost, enhancing focus and productivity.

Emotional Well-Being

Music is a powerful emotional regulator. It can evoke a wide range of emotions, from joy and excitement to nostalgia and tranquillity. For anyone navigating the complexities of life, music offers a safe space to process and express emotions. Whether it's a soothing classical piece or an upbeat pop song, music can uplift spirits and provide comfort during challenging times.

Stress Relief

In today's fast-paced world, stress is a common companion. However, music can be a potent antidote. Studies have shown that listening to calming music can lower cortisol levels. For those in high-pressure environments, taking a few moments to listen to relaxing music can significantly reduce stress and promote a sense of calm.

* * *

Rapper Divine's Life Story: A Symphony of Struggles and Success

Early Struggles

Born as Vivian Fernandes in the bustling city of Mumbai, Divine's early life was marked by hardship and adversity. Growing up in the slums, he faced numerous challenges, from financial difficulties to the absence of his parents. But amidst the chaos, Divine found solace in music.

The Impact of Music

Music became Divine's refuge and his voice. Influenced by international hip-hop artists, he began crafting his own rhymes, reflecting the grim realities of his life. His breakthrough came with the release of 'Yeh Mera Bombay', a raw and authentic portrayal of Mumbai's streets. This song resonated with many, catapulting him to fame and giving him a platform to share his story.

The movie *Gully Boy*, partly inspired by Divine's life, beautifully portrays how his journey is a testament to the transformative power of music. It not only helped him navigate his struggles but also empowered him to inspire others. Through his lyrics, Divine addresses social issues, giving a voice to the voiceless and highlighting the resilience of the human spirit.

* * *

Incorporating music into your daily routine can be a simple yet effective way to enhance your overall well-being. Whether you're a corporate professional seeking relief from stress, a student needing a mental boost, or simply someone looking for emotional comfort, music can be your ally.

Music is more than just a series of notes and rhythms; it's a universal language that speaks to the soul. Let it be a part of your journey, offering comfort, joy, and inspiration along the way.

Food for Thought

1. Which is your go-to comfort playlist or song that always make you feel better? What is so comforting about them?
2. Do you have a different playlist for different moods? How different do you feel with music?

Put Your Family First

BLESSED are those who have their families close to themselves. Do not ignore the importance of togetherness and the power that a strong family can fill you with. If you know someone who is away from his family, try and be the family for that person in whatever way you can. Trust me, you'll feel amazing.

When we try to build a life with our work or career in the centre, balancing everything around it, it is sure to shatter down. However, if we put our family in the centre and then build everything around it—our career, passions, hobbies—each aspect of our life is sure to flourish.

Easier said than done, but it is doable.

Conflicts exist in every family. As long as it doesn't make you lose sleep and peace of mind, it's better to resolve the conflict and relish in the togetherness. Bonding within the family is what children observe in their early years, and it's an important factor in their personality development.

* * *

David, a high-ranking executive in a multinational corporation, dedicated most of his time to climbing the corporate ladder. His demanding job required long hours, frequent travel, and constant connectivity. As a result, he spent very little time with his wife and two children.

Over the years, his absence took a toll on his family. His wife felt overwhelmed managing the household and children alone, leading to frequent arguments and emotional distance. His children, craving their father's attention, began to act out in school and at home. The lack of parental guidance and support affected their academic performance and self-esteem.

David's relentless focus on his career left him burnt out and emotionally detached. He missed out on important milestones in his children's lives, further straining their relationship. Eventually, the family reached a breaking point, with his wife filing for divorce and his children growing increasingly distant.

I'm pretty sure nobody would want success at this cost.

Now, let's consider the story of John, a successful entrepreneur. John's parents always made time to listen to his ideas and dreams, providing encouragement and constructive feedback. This support helped him develop a strong sense of self-worth and the courage to pursue his entrepreneurial ambitions. Even when faced with setbacks, John's family's unwavering belief in him kept his spirits high and motivated him to keep pushing forward. John carried on this system with his children as well, alongside pursuing his successful entrepreneurship career.

Home is where the heart is. The heart is where my home is.

This shows us that family is never a distraction from our dreams; they are the very foundation and roots of our dreams and career.

* * *

I've listened to the motivational speaker Les Brown's story about his family a million times. He and his twin brother were given away for adoption when they were just six weeks old. They were raised by a single mother who adopted them. Lesley used to think that they were abandoned right after birth until he had a paradigm shift when he started to believe that they were received by his adoptee mother with all the love in this world. He always took care of his mother, keeping her at the centre of all he did. His mother was the encouragement he needed in his most challenging hours—financially and professionally. He went on to become the Ohio State Legislature representative and an incredible motivational speaker. He even successfully fought cancer, because he wanted to be there for his son for as long as he could. His son gave him the inspiration to fight the most torturing illness ever.

The Obama Family

The Obama family is a prime example of how prioritising one's family can lead to personal and professional success. Despite the demands of his Presidency, Barack Obama always made time for his family. He often spoke about the importance of being present for his daughters, Malia and Sasha, ensuring that they grew up in a loving and supportive environment.

This commitment to family not only strengthened the Obamas' bond but also had a significant impact on the girls' development. They grew up to be confident, well-rounded individuals, demonstrating the benefits of a strong family foundation.

The Williams Sisters

Serena and Venus Williams, two of the greatest tennis players in history, owe much of their success to their family's support. Their parents, Richard and Oracene, dedicated themselves to their daughters' training and development from a young age. Their father's meticulous coaching and their mother's unwavering belief in their potential provided the sisters with the tools and confidence to excel.

The Williams family's commitment to each other and their shared goals exemplify how prioritising family can lead to extraordinary achievements. Serena and Venus often speak about the importance of their family's support in their success, highlighting the powerful impact of a strong family unit.

* * *

Putting your family first is not just about spending time together; it is about creating an environment that fosters emotional support, teaches values, and develops social skills. The examples of John, Maria, the Obama family, and the Williams sisters illustrate how a strong family foundation can lead to personal and professional success.

Prioritising family can have a lasting impact on an individual's personality and overall well-being. By nurturing and supporting each other, families can help their members achieve their full potential and navigate life's challenges with confidence and resilience. In a world that often pulls us in many directions, remembering to put your family first can be the key to a balanced and fulfilling life.

In addition to the examples mentioned, studies by National Institutes of Health (NIH) have also shown the positive effects of a strong family foundation on mental health. Research has found that individuals who come from supportive and loving families tend to have lower rates of anxiety and depression. This further emphasises the importance of prioritising family and creating a nurturing environment for personal well-being.

Furthermore, studies have shown that a strong family foundation can also have a positive impact on physical health. Research indicates that individuals who have strong family bonds and support systems tend to have lower rates of chronic illnesses and live longer, healthier lives. This highlights the holistic benefits of prioritising family and underscores the significance of nurturing familial relationships for overall well-being. By investing in our families, we not only cultivate personal success but also contribute to a healthier and happier society as a whole. Building a strong family foundation is essential for fostering a supportive and loving environment.

Tips to Build a Strong Family Foundation

Quality Time

- **Family Activities:** Engage in activities that everyone enjoys, such as game nights, outdoor adventures, or cooking together.
- **One-on-One Time:** Spend individual time with each family member to strengthen personal bonds.

Shared Responsibilities

- **Chore Rotation:** Create a chore chart to distribute household tasks evenly.
- **Teamwork:** Encourage working together on projects, which fosters a sense of teamwork and shared accomplishment.

Traditions and Rituals

- **Holiday Celebrations:** Establish and maintain family traditions during holidays and special occasions.
- **Daily Rituals:** Simple daily rituals, like having dinner together, can create a sense of stability and belonging.

Support and Encouragement

- **Positive Reinforcement:** Celebrate achievements and provide encouragement during challenging times.
- **Emotional Support:** Be there for each other emotionally, offering a shoulder to lean on when needed.

Healthy Conflict Resolution

- **Constructive Communication:** Address conflicts calmly and constructively, focusing on solutions rather than blaming each other.

- **Apology and Forgiveness:** Encourage apologising and forgiving to resolve disputes and move forward.

Just as it takes a village to raise a child, that very village (family) needs to be taken care of as well. It should be nurtured with conscious efforts, love, and affection to provide a positive environment for any child to be raised in.

Food for Thought

1. How is your bonding and equation within the family after you celebrate a festival or spend a holiday together?
2. Recall a time when your family had your back in a challenging or troubled situation and got you out of it.

The Habit of Happiness

YOU might be wondering how happiness can be a habit. Let me show you how.

Swati had been quite depressed and unhappy lately, but she knew not the reason why. Her life was perfectly fine—she was in a happy marriage and had a supportive family, she was doing pretty well at her job and building a career, and had two loving kids, each doing well at academics and other activities. Well, this was the image from an eagle's eye view. If we zoom in and view her life, we observe that she felt her better half didn't understand her work commitments, failing to provide much help in balancing the household responsibilities and work pressures. Even her relatives passed bitter comments on her ways of managing the household and spending less time with the kids. As a result, she got no breather and longed to feel free with no strings attached.

One fine day, she crossed paths with a school friend with whom she had lost touch. While chatting with her, she opened up about what she goes through on a daily basis.

Although she didn't want to make a huge fuss about it, these things impacted her, and she felt like she was just dragging her life. Her friend advised her to add one more thing to her list of responsibilities, prioritising it the most—happiness. Her statement stayed with Swati for quite a while, and she kept reflecting on it until she came up with some really creative solutions to make her life truly enjoyable. She blocked one day every month to go for a spa treatment, no matter what. This really relaxed her. She planned out her Sundays in advance to make the most of her available time with the kids, solidifying their bond. She stopped complaining to her husband and did everything with a smile, even laughing off the critical comments made by her relatives. This really changed her husband's attitude, and he became more loving and caring. He offered his support without being asked.

Swati made a change on the work-front too—she initiated some very courageous conversations with her superiors to implement certain improvement strategies and invest more in the well-being of the employees. This led to her getting a raise and a promotion. The only thing Swati changed was her mind-set, making her happiness her responsibility. Hence, what the Father of the Nation had once said stands true: **Be the change you wish to see in the world.**

* * *

Being happy is an expression. Well, why not make this expression a habit for yourself? Once you have the realisation that your happiness is your responsibility and not dependent on the actions of others, you will automatically be at peace and expect less—or nothing—from others. One of the main causes of our unhappiness is harbouring expectations from others. When these expectations are not met, we become upset and unhappy. It is very obvious and natural for expectations to not be met in most cases, especially in relationships, when they are not properly communicated. Expectations arise in our minds, and unless communicated, the other person can't have the slightest idea of them. It is wrong and unfair to assume that the other person will be aware of the expectations we have from them. Hence, the simplest key to happiness is to have little to no expectations from others and taking the onus on us to keep ourselves happy. One very effective statement made by one of my friends is: 'If I have ten reasons to upset me and make me unhappy, I make a conscious effort to find or create fifteen reasons to make me happy.' This statement drives me to take responsibility of my own happiness, because happy people really do have an edge over others.

The Benefits of Happiness

- Happy people are more successful as happiness boosts productivity.
- They are healthier because they experience positive emotions—they're calm, composed, and energetic. Happiness combats stress and anxiety.
- They have and maintain better relationships.
- They are more creative.
- They have better friends and a good social life.

- They are better leaders.

How to get into the habit of happiness?

- **Spend time with nature:** The tranquillity and beauty of natural surroundings can provide a sense of peace and rejuvenation, fostering a deeper connection to the world and a greater appreciation for life's simple pleasures.
- **Learn to forgive:** Forgiveness can free individuals from the burden of anger and resentment, leading to emotional healing and inner peace. By letting go of grudges, people can experience more positive emotions, improved relationships, and a greater sense of happiness. By forgiving, you do yourself a big favour.
- **Make a life list** (and make some efforts to keep checking off the items in the list): Creating and pursuing a life list (or bucket list) provide a sense of purpose and direction. Achieving personal goals and experiencing new adventures can bring joy, fulfilment, and a sense of accomplishment, all of which contribute to happiness.
- **Learn a new hobby:** Engaging in a new hobby can be a source of joy and relaxation. It provides opportunities for creativity, skill development, and social interaction, all of which can enhance self-esteem and overall happiness.
- **Embrace your fears:** Facing and overcoming fears can build confidence and resilience. It allows

individuals to grow and expand their comfort zones, leading to new opportunities and experiences that can bring a sense of achievement and happiness.

- **Move out of your comfort zone (do something challenging):** Challenging oneself by stepping out of the comfort zone can lead to personal growth and new experiences. This gives a sense of accomplishment and excitement, contributing to a richer and more fulfilling life.
- **Volunteer for some social service:** Volunteering provides a sense of purpose and connection to others. Helping those in need can increase feelings of empathy, compassion, and gratitude, leading to greater happiness and life satisfaction.

The Habit of Being Happy: Taking Responsibility for Your Own Good

Happiness is not just a fleeting emotion but a habit, a responsibility we owe to ourselves. It's about making conscious choices every day to cultivate a life filled with joy and contentment. Let's find out how self-care, positive thinking, and mindfulness can help you take charge of your happiness, inspired by the lives of famous personalities.

Self-Care: Nurturing Your Well-Being

Self-care is foundational to happiness. It's about taking time to nurture your body, mind, and soul. Milind Soman, an Indian supermodel, actor, film producer, and fitness enthusiast is a strong advocate for self-care, fitness, and healthy living. He is known for his dedication to maintaining a healthy lifestyle and often shares his fitness journey and wellness tips through social media and public appearances.

Remember the famous quote by Oprah Winfrey: **Breathe. Let go. And remind yourself that this very moment is the only one you know you have for sure.**

By prioritising self-care, you can create a solid foundation for a happy life. Whether it's through exercise, a balanced diet, or by simply taking out time to relax, self-care is a powerful tool in your happiness toolkit.

Positive Thinking: Shaping Your Reality

'I am fundamentally an optimist. Whether that comes from nature or nurture, I cannot say. Part of being optimistic is keeping one's head pointed toward the sun, one's feet moving forward.' – Nelson Mandela.

Positive thinking is about seeing the good in every situation and believing in the best possible outcome. Nelson Mandela, the former President of South Africa, exemplified positive thinking even during his twenty-seven years in prison. He maintained his optimism and hope for a better future, which eventually led to the end of apartheid and his emergence as a global symbol of resilience and peace.

By adopting a positive mind-set, you can transform your challenges into opportunities and create a more fulfilling life. It's about training your mind to focus on the positive aspects of life, no matter the circumstances.

Mindfulness: Living in the Present

Mindfulness is the practice of being fully present in the moment, aware of where we are and what we're doing. It helps us to appreciate the here and now, reducing stress and enhancing our overall happiness. Steve Jobs, the co-founder of Apple, was a strong advocate of mindfulness. He practised Zen Buddhism and often spoke about the importance of living in the moment. He said, 'Your work is going to fill a large part of your life, and the only way to be truly satisfied is to do what you believe is great work. And the only way to do great work is to love what you do. If you haven't found it yet, keep looking. Don't settle.'

Incorporating mindfulness into your daily routine can help you stay grounded, reduce anxiety, and increase your appreciation for life's simple pleasures.

***

Children are the best teachers of the habit of happiness—just observe them whenever they're around. It doesn't really take much for them to be happy. They find happiness in an open field, running in joy, enjoying the rain, watching their favourite cartoon, or just jumping around and dancing without music. Even when they get upset over something, they have a tendency to forget and move on after mere minutes. That's something I really wish I had retained as we grew up, because certain grudges and unwanted memories become our unwanted baggage. So, let's adopt a child's mind-set to embrace the happiness we observe in every particle around us and leave behind any grudges to travel light in this journey.

Happiness is a habit that requires effort and commitment. By focusing on self-care, positive thinking, and mindfulness, you can take responsibility for your own happiness. Remember, it's not about waiting for happiness to find you but creating it yourself.

Start today by making small changes in your routine.

Resource

1. Read *Happiness: How to get into the Habit of being Happy* by Gill Hasson.

Call to Action

1. Consciously pick a day when you decide to switch off the 'complaining' mode and be happy for whatever comes your way. At the end of the day, journal the differences you note.
2. Strategically block some time in your day devoted to something that makes you happy—reading, singing, playing a sport, or going for a walk.

Food for Thought

1. Think about the last time you consciously did something to make yourself happy.
2. Do you take responsibility for your own happiness?

THOUGHT BREAK

What's your BIG task?

The Power of Breaking Down Big Goals.

Have you ever felt overwhelmed by a massive goal or a long period of time stretching out before you? It's easy to get bogged down by the sheer scale of it all.

But what if you could break it down into smaller, manageable pieces?

That's the beauty of division! By breaking down big goals or chunks of time into smaller tasks or shorter intervals, you can:

- Create a sense of control and momentum
- Focus on one task at a time, avoiding feeling overwhelmed
- Celebrate small wins, boosting motivation and confidence
- Make steady progress, leading to significant accomplishments

Try it with your next big goal or project

- Divide it into smaller tasks or milestones
- Set specific deadlines for each task
- Focus on one task at a time
- Celebrate each small win

Watch your progress add up to achieve something truly remarkable!

Remember, big goals are achieved one small step at a time. Break them down, stay focused, and keep moving forward!

The Power of Affirmations

GAUR Gopal Das, a former Hewlett-Packard engineer turned monk, is a renowned Indian motivational speaker and author who actively promotes the power of affirmations. Through his extensive social media presence, public talks, and his book *Life's Amazing Secrets*, he shares personal experiences and practical advice on incorporating positive affirmations into our daily lives to cultivate a positive mind-set, overcome challenges, and achieve personal goals. His teachings have inspired countless individuals to embrace affirmations as a tool for enhancing mental and emotional well-being.

What are affirmations?

Affirmations are specific positive statements that help in building positivity and overcoming negative thoughts. So, how do these positive statements help us as a powerful and impactful habit?

What we keep repeating to ourselves stays in our mind longer, and what lingers in our mind consistently is what we experience in our lives. It's a form of the law of attraction. That's how affirmations work. It's an exercise for the brain. Similar to exercise, affirmations increase the levels of feel-good hormones. Moreover, just like the results of exercise are revealed only if done regularly and consistently, affirmations too require regularity and consistency to have a lasting and life-changing impact. The power of affirmations makes us realise the actual strength of words. The effect might be mild at first, but over time these affirmations will help to create a more meaningful and positive existence.

What does research have to say about affirmations?

Studies show that when self-affirmation activities are performed, the ventromedial prefrontal cortex, involved in positive valuation and self-related information processing, becomes more active.

Louise Hay, an American author, was a living example of how to completely transform your life with the power of positive affirmations. After going through physical abuse in her early childhood and a divorce later, she was diagnosed with incurable cervical cancer. At that point, refusing the conventional medical treatments, Louise discovered non-medical healing alternatives through forgiveness, affirmations, and dietary health. She not only overcame the cancer but lived till the age of ninety. There are numerous books she has written on affirmations and especially their healing power.

Affirmations are encouragement for the self, and as we know, it goes a long way in bringing positive results. Affirmations can be another keystone habit as this helps in building other good habits and making our positive thoughts actionable.

Benefits of Positive Affirmations

- Self-affirmations help to reduce stress and anxiety.
- Affirmations help in healing the body from diseases.
- They help in achieving better grades.
- It helps in better sleep as it relaxes the otherwise restless mind.
- Affirmations encourage an optimistic mind-set and personality.
- It helps in building positive habits.
- Affirmations help in overcoming the ghosts of the past.

Tips and Tricks to Practise Daily

- Start your mornings with affirmations—repeat them to yourself or play them on your phone with earphones on.
- Repeat the affirmations few times a day.
- Do mindful breathing after you say the affirmations.
- Practise saying affirmations whenever any negative thought comes to your mind.

What should be your affirmations?

They can be anything simple and positive depending on the phase of life you are in. There are many websites, mobile applications, and books which list out the different affirmations to be used as per your requirement. These include affirmations for teenagers and kids, and even to fight depression, relieve stress, be successful, and likewise.

So, to conclude, every resource you need to accomplish anything and lead your life by design rather than default are in your mind. Understand the limitless powers of your mind and tap that potential with affirmations. Use a powerful affirmation as your 'power mantra' throughout the day. Make it an influential self-talk that fills you up with self-belief, leaving no room for self-doubt.

Resources

1. Read *Mirror Work: 21 Days to Heal Your Life* by Louise Hay.

Call to Action

Design your personal power mantra and repeat it to yourself. It could be something as simple as, 'I am better than the best' or 'I am loved' or 'I am happy and successful'.

Food for Thought

1. Have you ever tried affirmations before? If yes, did you notice any changes?
2. If you have never tried affirmations, are you willing to try them now?
3. What, according to you, will be your key affirmations?

The Meditation Revolution

WHAT made me adopt the habit of meditation so strongly was completely accidental.

Once while scrolling through Netflix, I bumped into a documentary named *Headspace—A Guide to Meditation.* It is a short-animated series but really impactful. It compelled me try this practice of meditating.

So, I started with short guided meditations, starting just with five minutes every morning. As soon as I woke up, I put on a small five-minute meditation video on YouTube and connected my earphones, closed my eyes and there I was, in a completely different world.

Yes, the human mind, akin to the antics of a monkey, wandered at first, but slowly and gradually, with each passing day, it got better.

What got even better unknowingly was the quality of my days—they were calmer and more controlled. Things somehow just worked out for me.

And as I kept experimenting with different meditation methods, I came across Vishen Lakhiani's Six Phase Meditation method, and till date I practise that.

Let's have a brief look at Vishen's story.

Imagine a young entrepreneur, stressed, overworked, and on the brink of burnout. This was Vishen Lakhiani before he discovered the life-changing habit of meditation. Little did he know that this ancient practice would not only save his sanity but also catapult him to unprecedented levels of personal and professional success.

The Breaking Point

Vishen's life before meditation was a whirlwind of ambition and stress. Working in the Silicon Valley, he was constantly pushing himself to the limit, believing that success came from relentless hustle. However, this approach was sure to take a toll.

'I was running on empty,' Vishen recalls. 'My relationships were suffering, my health was deteriorating, and despite working eighteen-hour days, I wasn't growing as I had hoped.'

It was at this low point that Vishen stumbled upon meditation. Sceptical at first, he decided to give it a try out of sheer desperation.

The Meditation Revolution

From the moment Vishen began his meditation practice, he noticed subtle shifts in his life. 'It wasn't an overnight transformation,' he explains. 'But gradually, I found myself becoming calmer, more focused, and surprisingly, more productive.'

As Vishen delved deeper into his practice, he experienced what he describes as a 'personal revolution'. His stress levels plummeted, his creativity soared, and he found himself making better decisions, both in his personal life and business.

Meditation: The Secret Weapon for Business Success

Perhaps the most surprising outcome of Vishen's meditation journey was its impact on his business. As his mind became clearer and more focused, Mindvalley began to flourish.

'Meditation gave me the mental clarity to see opportunities I had been missing,' Vishen shares. 'It helped me attract and retain top talent, make better strategic decisions, and create a company culture that truly resonated with our mission.'

Under Vishen's meditation-enhanced leadership, Mindvalley grew to become a global leading platform in personal growth education, impacting millions of lives worldwide.

Overcoming Challenges Through Mindfulness

Vishen's journey wasn't without its challenges. There were times when the pressure to perform threatened to derail his newfound peace. However, his meditation practice provided him with the tools to navigate these obstacles with grace and resilience.

'Meditation taught me to observe my thoughts and emotions without getting caught up in them,' Vishen explains. 'This allowed me to respond to challenges from a place of calm clarity rather than reactive stress.'

The Six Phase Meditation: Vishen's Gift to the World

As Vishen's practice deepened, he began to develop his own unique approach to meditation. This culminated in the creation of the Six Phase Meditation technique, a powerful practice that combines multiple aspects of personal growth into one comprehensive daily ritual.

The Six Phase Meditation includes:

Compassion, Gratitude, Forgiveness, Future Dreaming, Perfect Day, Blessing.

'This technique is designed to not only calm the mind but also to actively shape your reality,' Vishen explains. 'It's about creating a positive mind-set, setting intentions, and aligning yourself with your highest goals.'

The effects of meditation are far-reaching, positively impacting our physical health and our mental wellness, including cognitive functioning and emotional control.

Benefits of Meditation

Studies show that regular meditation helps to reduce:

- Anxiety
- Depression
- Stress levels

- Job burnout

We also see psychological benefits, such as:

- Heightened empathy
- Improved interoceptive awareness (stimuli and sensations within the body)
- Better psychological well-being
- Increased self-directedness (awareness that our actions and behaviours reflect our choices)
- Improved cooperativeness (degree of agreeableness in relationships with others)
- More self-transcendence (rising above the self and relating to something bigger)

To summarise, start with five minutes of guided meditation. There are endless resources available online. Choose a space and time that suits you best. Be consistent for seven days and observe for improvements. Even the slightest noticeable positive change makes it worth it to continue.

Resources

1. Goodful's (YouTube channel) meditation videos.
2. *Meditation for Beginners* by Jack Kornfield.
3. *Silva Method of Meditation.*

Food for Thought

1. Have you practised meditation before? If yes, what changes did you see in yourself?
2. What would be your key takeaways from this chapter?

THOUGHT BREAK

What's your best reaction under pressure?

In times of turmoil, talent and knowledge are essential, but temperament is the real differentiator.

Remember the 'Miracle on the Hudson' in 2009? Captain Chesley Sullenberger's exceptional temperament saved 155 lives when his plane's engines failed.

(Watch the movie *Sully* if you haven't.)

In this life-or-death situation, Sullenberger's temperament played a crucial role.

He remained calm and composed, which helped him think clearly and make rational decisions.

He stayed focused on the task at hand, prioritising the safety of all 155 passengers and crew.

He drew on his extensive experience to quickly assess the situation and choose the best course of action.

He communicated clearly and confidently with his crew and passengers, instilling trust and reassurance.

He made quick and decisive decisions, including the controversial decision to land the plane on the river.

Thanks to his exceptional temperament, the plane landed safely on the Hudson River, and all people on board were rescued. The incident became known as the 'Miracle on the Hudson'.

Sullenberger's story is a powerful reminder that temperament matters, especially in testing times.

Monitor Your Food Habits

THROUGHOUT my student life, I hardly ever paid any attention to the food I ate. My favourite indulgences were noodles, pastas, dim sums, burgers, fried food—basically anything and everything that wasn't home-cooked and satisfied my taste buds. Our college life is when we tend to spend most of our time hanging out with friends and having the cheapest foods from the most accessible and close-by food streets. Those late-night Maggis felt like bowls of bliss.

The very first time I paid close attention to my eating habits was when I was expecting and my doctor gave me a long list of what to and what not to eat. I became very careful that time, since I was now responsible for the life inside me. I drastically cut down on my tea intake as well. Being a tea lover through and through, it was something I never thought I'd be able to do.

Without failure, each day I consumed nuts, fruits, veggies, proteins, and seeds. With changes in my diet, I saw a change in my everyday life—my moods, actions, responses to everything, and my energy levels. Yes, diet isn't just for your physical looks, it goes beyond that.

In the pursuit of health and wellness, the importance of a balanced diet cannot be overstated. Eating a variety of foods from all food groups ensures that we get the necessary nutrients to fuel our bodies and minds. This chapter delves into the significance of balanced nutrition and illustrates this with real-life examples that highlight the transformative power of a well-rounded diet.

In order to have a balanced diet, first and foremost, awareness about your body and its unique needs are important. Hence, a regular annual or a semi-annual health check-up is necessary to find out about any specific deficiencies that might require attention.

I got to know that I was Beta Thalassemia Minor, which meant my body's production of haemoglobin is low. Hence, my diet should always include iron-rich foods to compensate for this deficiency.

There are many such other things which we mightn't know about ourselves unless we get a health test done. Hence, please take it seriously and then plan your diet if you want to save on medical bills later.

The Foundation of a Balanced Diet

A balanced diet includes a mix of carbohydrates, proteins, fats, vitamins, and minerals. The goal is not just to consume calories but to intake a variety of nutrients that help our bodies function optimally. The benefits of such a diet are manifold, including enhanced energy levels, improved brain function, stronger immune systems, and a lower risk of chronic diseases.

The Science Behind Nutritional Balance

Nutritional science shows that diverse diets help to prevent malnutrition in all its forms, as well as a range of non-communicable diseases and conditions. The body's complex needs cannot be met by a single food or food group, making variety a key component of good nutrition.

How to Cultivate the Habit of Balanced Eating?

Plan Your Meals

Begin by planning your meals for the week. This ensures a variety of food groups are included and reduces the temptation to opt for less healthy and convenient food options due to time constraints.

Educate Yourself

Understanding what constitutes a balanced diet is crucial. Utilise resources like the USDA's MyPlate or consult with a dietitian to learn about the proportions and types of food that should be included in your diet.

Make Gradual Changes

Transition to a balanced diet gradually to ensure sustainable changes. Start by introducing more vegetables and fruits, swapping refined grains for whole grains, and choosing lean protein sources.

Impact of a Balanced Diet

Revitalization of a Corporate Executive

Sarah, a high-level executive in a bustling New York firm, found herself constantly fatigued and stressed. Her meals were often quick grabs: pastries for breakfast, fast food for lunch, and sometimes skipping dinner or settling for instant noodles. After consulting a nutritionist, Sarah began incorporating a variety of whole foods into her diet, such as fruits, vegetables, whole grains, and lean proteins. The change was dramatic. Within weeks, she reported higher energy levels, better focus at work, and improved sleep quality. Her example led to the initiation of a Healthy Meal Program at her workplace, encouraging all employees to adopt similar dietary changes.

Transformation of a Diabetic Patient

John, a fifty-year-old diagnosed with Type 2 diabetes, faced severe health warnings from his doctor. His diet was rich in processed foods and sugary drinks, contributing to his condition. Under the guidance of a dietitian, John adopted a balanced diet that included fibre-rich vegetables, fruits, and controlled portions of whole grains, alongside regular physical activity. Over six months, not only did his blood sugar levels stabilise without reliance on high medication doses but he also lost excess weight and lowered his risk of cardiovascular diseases.

Improved Academic Performance in School Children

A public school in Oregon implemented a new lunch program that focused on balanced diets, replacing heavily processed foods with fresh, local produce and balanced nutrients. Teachers and parents noticed a marked improvement in the students' attention spans, academic performance, and overall behaviour. This initiative was so successful that it was adopted by all the schools in the district, showcasing the direct impact of nutrition on cognitive function and learning in children.

In a country like India, where poverty and malnutrition are common, it becomes awfully difficult for malnourished students to do academically well. This is the most basic need, and we should be serious about spreading its awareness everywhere, implementing healthy eating habits wherever we can. Let's choose to be grateful for the food on our tables and mindful about our eating habits. Your unwanted anger might just be more than work stress.

Adopting a balanced diet is a transformative journey that enhances physical, mental, and emotional health. The real-life examples in this chapter illustrate just how profound these changes can be. By making mindful choices about the food we consume, we not only improve our own health but also set a positive example for those around us. In the symphony of life, a balanced diet is the music that lets our bodies dance with vitality and vigour.

Food for Thought

1. Have you ever been on a diet? What impact did that have on your body and other aspects of your routine?
2. What are the top three changes that you'd want to introduce in your daily diet after reading this chapter?

Embrace the Unknown

The biggest risk is not taking any risk . . . In a world that is changing really quickly, the only strategy that is guaranteed to fail is not taking risks. – Mark Zuckerberg.

IMAGINE standing at the edge of a cliff, the wind whipping around you and the ground far below. The leap seems daunting yet exhilarating. This is what risk-taking feels like. It's the thrill of the unknown, the promise of potential success, and the fear of failure all wrapped into one. But why is this leap so crucial, especially when it comes to making significant decisions?

As someone with very humble beginnings, leaving the safety net and leaping into the unknown has not been a common phenomenon around me. What has been common is having a safe and secure job, not travelling to unexplored destinations as they are unknown, and always following the crowd because it is tried and tested, synonymous to 'safe'. Since our previous generations went

Fear is the price you pay for sweet victory.

through a lot of struggles, having seen the wars, Partition, riots, and what not, all this hardly left any appetite for risk. However, things changed with the next generations which saw industrialisation, privatisation, and globalisation. This generation has been exposed to a world of opportunities and hence a greater risk appetite.

The Crucial Role of Risk-Taking

Risk-taking is the heartbeat of innovation and progress. Without it, we'll remain stagnant, never pushing the boundaries of what's possible. For young professionals, students, and business leaders, the ability to take calculated risks can be the difference between mediocrity and greatness. It's about stepping out of your comfort zone and daring to chase dreams that seem out of reach.

Real-Life Stories: Lessons from the Bold

Elon Musk: The Maverick Entrepreneur

Musk's journey is a testament to the power of risk-taking. From co-founding PayPal to launching SpaceX and Tesla, Musk has consistently bet on the future. When SpaceX faced multiple rocket failures, many doubted the viability of private space travel. But Musk's unwavering belief and willingness to risk everything paid off. Today, SpaceX is a leader in space exploration, and Tesla has revolutionised the automobile industry.

Athletes Who Dared to Dream

Consider Michael Jordan, widely regarded as one of the greatest basketball players of all time. Before his six NBA championships, Jordan faced numerous setbacks, including being rejected from his high school basketball team. Instead of giving up, he took the risk of pushing harder, training longer, and believing in his potential. His story is a powerful reminder that risks can lead to extraordinary success.

Overcoming the Fear of Taking Risks

Fear is the biggest barrier to taking risks. It's natural to fear the unknown, but overcoming this fear is essential. Here are some strategies:

- **Embrace Failure as a Learning Opportunity:** Understand that failure is not the end but a stepping stone to success. Each failure provides valuable lessons that bring you closer to your goals.
- **Start Small:** Begin with smaller risks to build confidence. As you experience success, take on more significant challenges gradually.
- **Surround Yourself with Supportive People:** Having a network of mentors and peers who encourage and support you can make a world of difference.

Strategic Decision-Making: Calculated Risks

Taking risks doesn't mean being reckless. It's about making informed decisions and weighing the potential outcomes. Here are some tips for strategic risk-taking:

- **Research and Plan:** Gather as much information as possible before making a decision. A well-researched plan reduces uncertainty.
- **Evaluate the Pros and Cons:** Consider the potential benefits and drawbacks. This helps in making balanced decisions.
- **Trust Your Instincts:** Sometimes, intuition can guide you in the right direction. Trust your gut feeling, especially when it aligns with your research.

Embrace the Journey

Risk-taking is not just about the outcome but the journey. It's about growth, learning, and pushing the boundaries of what's possible. As you navigate your path, remember that every significant achievement starts with a leap of faith.

So, take that leap. Embrace the unknown. Dare to dream big, and let the habit of risk-taking propel you to new heights.

Resources

1. Read *Choose Possibility: How to Master Risks and Thrive* by Sukhinder Singh Cassidy.

Food for Thought

1. Have you ever taken a small, calculated risk where you were mentally prepared for the worst? For example, exploring a new restaurant on a friend's recommendation and coming back disappointed?
2. How about trying an adventure sport with friends, something you have never been comfortable about? *(Do you recall a similar Bollywood movie with this theme?)*

THOUGHT BREAK

Show up, even if every cell of yours feels reluctant about it.

In life and business, showing up is an underrated but crucial skill. There will be moments when we have no clear sense of direction, no immediate solutions, and no grand strategies to implement. During these times, simply showing up can make all the difference.

By being present, we signal our commitment and resilience. We demonstrate that even in uncertainty, we are willing to engage, learn, and contribute.

Showing up allows us to be a part of the conversation, to observe and understand the dynamics at play, and to gradually find our way.

Sometimes, the most significant breakthroughs come not from having all the answers but from the act of being there—ready to listen, support, and act when the time is right.

Remember, it's not always about knowing the path ahead but having the courage to step forward, one moment at a time.

So, next time you feel lost or unsure, just show up. Your presence alone can create opportunities and pave the way to success.

Log Out

In today's hyper-connected world, the buzz of smartphones, glow of screens, and constant flow of information can feel inescapable. Our lives revolve around digital notifications, social media updates, and the relentless pulse of the internet. However, cultivating the habit of turning off technology, even for brief periods, can yield profound benefits for our mental health, relationships, and productivity. This chapter explores the importance of this habit and provides real-life examples to illustrate its positive impacts.

Understanding the Need to Disconnect

The digital age, while bringing the world closer, has also blurred the lines between work and home, public and private life. This omnipresence of technology can lead to digital fatigue, a phenomenon where the constant engagement with digital devices leads to burnout, stress, and a decrease in productivity. Moreover, several studies have linked excessive technology use with increased feelings of anxiety, depression, and even sleep disturbances.

The Science Behind Unplugging

Research suggests that detaching from digital devices can help to reset our biological clock, reduce stress, and improve interpersonal relationships. The blue light emitted by screens interferes with the production of melatonin, the hormone responsible for regulating sleep. By turning off our devices an hour before bed, we can enhance the quality of our sleep, thus improving our overall health and well-being.

The Benefits of Unplugging

Enhanced Creativity at a Technology Giant

At a leading technology company in Silicon Valley, a policy of 'No-Tech Tuesdays' was implemented where employees were encouraged to spend their breaks without any form of digital devices. This initiative led to an unexpected surge in creativity. Employees reported feeling more relaxed and open to new ideas. The informal chats by the water cooler and face-to-face interactions sparked creative solutions that hadn't emerged in the typical, plugged-in brainstorming sessions.

Improved Family Relationships

Consider the story of the Thompson family from New Jersey. They implemented a 'digital detox' rule during their meals, which was initially met with resistance, especially from the teenagers. However, over time, this practice helped family members engage more deeply with each other, sharing stories, challenges, and laughter without the distraction of buzzing phones. This not only strengthened their emotional bonds but also improved their overall satisfaction with family life.

Increased Productivity in Academia

A professor at a prominent university started encouraging students to turn off their laptops and phones during lectures. Initially, students were sceptical, believing it would hinder their note-taking abilities. However, they soon found that this practice helped them focus better and retain more information. The quality of classroom discussions improved, and students reported a better understanding of complex concepts without the transitory aid of technology.

How to Cultivate the Habit of Unplugging?

Set Specific Times

Start by designating tech-free times in your daily routine. This could be during meals, the first hour after waking up, or the hour before going to bed. The key is being consistent and making these tech-free times a predictable part of your day.

Create Tech-Free Zones

Designate certain areas of your home, such as the dining room or bedrooms, as tech-free zones. These spaces can foster non-digital activities like reading, meditating, or engaging in deep conversations.

Engage in Non-Digital Activities

Replace the time you would typically spend on devices with activities that don't require technology, such as walking, reading a physical book, or practising a hobby like cooking or painting.

Turning off technology, even for short periods, can significantly enhance our lives. It allows us to reclaim our time, improve our mental health, and deepen our relationships with others and ourselves. By consciously choosing to unplug, we can resist the tide of digital overwhelm and create a more balanced and fulfilling life. By embracing the art of unplugging, we find not what we lose, but what we gain.

A TED talk by seven-year-old Molly Wright is an eye opener. She demonstrates how a simple act like parents' scrolling on their phone in front of their children can adversely impact their growth and responses. It's a must watch for every parent who truly wants to invest in their child's growth. While it's impossible to completely cut off technology, limiting it and having certain time boundaries is definitely within our control.

In the recent times, it has been absolutely disheartening to see young teens falling prey to online adventures like the Blue Whale challenge, which requires children to physically hurt themselves, eventually attempting suicide. Hence, the need to control the use of technology rather than getting controlled by it is urgent and requires immediate attention.

Call to Action

Put your phone away for at least ninety minutes after waking up. Do not look at any notifications, mails, or messages.

1. Consciously plan some time for digital detox over the weekend and indulge in 'offline' activities you enjoy or spend time with family and friends.

Food for Thought

1. Do you practise logging off and minimising screen time before sleeping at night?
2. What is your average screen time? If it is high, will you take proactive measures to reduce it?
3. What other activities can you do during the time you're away from your phone?

The Early Bird Takes the Worm

I WAS never a morning person, but I have always wanted to be one.

Everything I tried to build a morning habit was rather short-lived—only a day—and the next day I snoozed again.

So, this was when I had no choice left. When my daughter was six months old and hooked to me from the moment I got up, it left me with no washroom breaks in peace without her crying and banging on the door. This was very frustrating and it left me very irritable and cranky. This eventually came out on my poor little girl.

More than anything in life, I have always been a peace-seeker. I always look for peaceful destinations to travel to, peaceful hotels or resorts to stay in, and peaceful spaces in office or home to work in. Just to get that few minutes of peace, I started to wake up fifteen minutes earlier than my daughter every day, which was enough for me to use the washroom peacefully. How? I think it was the 'mother clock' plus the 'body clock' and some help with my phone alarm.

Those fifteen minutes became the best part of my day, giving me some time to relax, reflect, and plan my day. These fifteen minutes grew to thirty and I enjoyed them thoroughly. I was also able to build in a fifteen-minutes yoga routine in it. Gradually, when my daughter grew old enough to go to play school and then a formal school, this time grew to an hour. I had to push the time a little earlier to accommodate her school time, that is, from 6 a.m. to 5 a.m., when her formal schooling started. But it was an enjoyable process, and since I had been looking forward to it, it wasn't painful for me to do so.

Thus, this head start made me 1% better each day with all the things I was able to do in that early hour—from meditation and yoga to writing and listening to Ted talks. Now, it's a habit to be proud of, something I understand the value of.

Getting an early start to the day is as important as getting an early start in other aspects of our lives, such as a career or a project. Also, the best time to start is right now.

The Power of an Early Start: Building a Foundation for Success

In today's fast-paced world, the value of an early start can never be overstated. Whether it's about launching a career, like Sachin Tendulkar debuting at sixteen, Ed Sheeran writing his songs at the tender age of eleven, or beginning a learning journey early, the benefits of being the early bird are immense. The secret lies in taking small, consistent steps every day, starting with the simple act of waking up early and taking charge of your day.

For Professionals: Setting the Tone for Success

For professionals, an early start sets a proactive tone for the day. Rising early allows for uninterrupted time to plan, reflect, and prepare. This habit not only boosts productivity but also enhances mental clarity and reduces stress. Starting your day with a clear plan can lead to more efficient work and a greater sense of accomplishment by the end of the day.

Practical Tips for Professionals

- **Create a Morning Routine:** Spend the first hour of your day planning tasks, setting goals, and prioritising activities.
- **Exercise:** Incorporate physical activity to boost energy and focus.
- **Learn Continuously:** Dedicate time each morning to read industry news, learn new skills, or engage in professional development.

For Students: Building a Foundation for Lifelong Learning

Students who start their learning journey early develop a strong foundation for academic and personal growth.

Waking up early and dedicating time to study and self-improvement can foster discipline, enhance cognitive function, and improve academic performance.

Practical Tips for Students

- **Establish Study Habits:** Use the early hours for focused study sessions, free from distractions.
- **Set Daily Goals:** Break down larger academic goals into manageable daily tasks.
- **Engage in Enriching Activities:** Use the extra time for reading, practising a hobby, or exploring new interests.

For Homemakers: Creating a Harmonious Routine

For homemakers, an early start provides precious moments of solitude and preparation before the household wakes up. This time can be used for personal well-being, planning household tasks, and setting a positive tone for the day.

Practical Tips for Homemakers

- **Self-Care:** Use the quiet morning hours for meditation, exercise, or enjoying a peaceful breakfast.
- **Organise the Day:** Plan meals, activities, and household chores early to avoid last-minute stress.

- **Personal Growth:** Spend time on a hobby, learning new skills, or engaging in personal development activities.

The Ripple Effect of an Early Start

The benefits of starting early extend beyond the individual. When professionals, students, and homemakers adopt this practice, it creates a positive ripple effect on families, workplaces, and communities. Early risers often exhibit better time management, increased productivity, and a greater sense of well-being, setting an inspiring example for others.

So, identify your trigger first. For example, getting a peaceful washroom time was mine. A trigger that is strong enough to get you an early start; a trigger that is non-negotiable for you; a trigger that is just for you. Once you identify it, use it to get you going!

An early start in life, career, or daily routine can lead to significant long-term benefits. By embracing the habit of waking up early and taking small, consistent steps each day, we can build a strong foundation for success. Whether you're a professional seeking to enhance your career, a student aiming for academic excellence, or a homemaker striving for a harmonious household, the power of an early start can transform your life.

Remember, it all begins with a single step each day. Wake up early, take charge, and watch how your life unfolds in extraordinary ways.

Food for Thought

1. Are you an early riser? What do you like most about those quiet hours?
2. What do you usually do during that time?
3. If you aren't an early riser, why so? What changes can you make in your lifestyle to become an early riser?

The Five Minutes' Rule

HAVING the patience to spend time on healthy habits like exercising, reading, or walking becomes practically difficult especially when you have a highly demanding job, are a parent, or a caregiver to elderly parents. We know the benefits of these healthy habits and even want to do all. But it becomes difficult when time isn't on our side, whether it is to rise early to prepare lunch for children, get them ready for school, do the chores, get ready for work, attend the never-ending schedules, calls, deadlines, and a chaotic evening with dinner demands and your ongoing work calls. And even if you don't have any family responsibilities, the nature of our corporate work life is such that we tend to think about our work all day long, which in itself becomes overwhelming.

In such a situation, the ultimate hack is to take out five minutes. Yes, five minutes. Borrow these from your sleep, commuting time, or any small break in your day.

The Power of Five Minutes

Identify five minutes in your day just for yourself, free from any distractions or obligations. Here's how you can make the most of these precious moments:

Morning Mindfulness

- **Sky Before the Screen:** Right after you wake up, avoid reaching for your phone. Instead, look out of the window, step outside, or find a peaceful spot to simply observe the sky and nature around you.
- **Meditation:** Spend these five minutes meditating. Set a timer if needed, and focus on deep breathing or a short-guided meditation from platforms like YouTube. You may put on a timer for five minutes, but only if you can do so without getting distracted by other notifications.
- **Practise Gratitude:** Use these moments to express gratitude. Reflect on the new day, the fresh air, and the presence of loved ones.
- **Affirmations:** Recite powerful affirmations like 'I am strong', 'I am at peace', or 'I am confident'. Regular practice can significantly enhance your mind-set.

Daytime Breaks

- **Commute Time:** Transform your commute by listening to an audiobook, TED talk, or motivational speaker. If reading is an option, immerse yourself in a book, be it fiction or self-help. Les Brown, Mel Robbins, Jay Shetty—all of them have been commuting with me via audiobooks ever since and making not only my commute but also my days and life better.

- **Movement:** During your workday, take five-minute breaks to stand, stretch, breathe deeply, and drink water. This can rejuvenate you and enhance productivity.

Evening Wind-Down

- **Pre-Bed Rituals:** Conclude your day with five minutes of gratitude, reading, affirmations, or meditation. These practices can improve your sleep quality and overall well-being

Making It Work for You

The key is to choose five minutes that fit seamlessly into your routine. Whether it's early in the morning, during a break, or before bed, these small, intentional acts can have profound impact. Even on the busiest days, you can carve out time for yourself, fostering better mental and physical health.

You are the ultimate benefiter of these five minutes—you decide and choose which habit will make you feel good, and just do that.

Remember, it's not about overhauling your entire schedule, but integrating small, consistent habits that promote well-being. By dedicating just five minutes to mindfulness, gratitude, or movement, you'll gradually build resilience and a more balanced lifestyle.

Call to Action

Incorporating healthy habits doesn't require hours of your day. Start with just five minutes. These moments of self-care can significantly improve your quality of life, making you more resilient, focused, and content. Embrace the five-minute hack and transform your busy lifestyle, one small habit at a time.

Food for Thought

1. If you were to apply the five minutes' rule from today, what would you choose to do during that time?

THOUGHT BREAK

Are We Just Going Through Life, or Growing Through Life?

Ever thought about how life happens in our waking hours? What we do with those precious moments defines us. Right now, are you living it to the fullest, or stuck in a cycle of regret?

You can choose to be grateful or spend those precious hours complaining. Remember, even coffee needs a little bit of grind to get that perfect brew.

You can decide to be productive or a master procrastinator. Ever noticed how 'later' can quickly turn into 'never'?

You can opt to be giving or spend your time grieving. Think of life as a boomerang–what you throw out there will come back to you!

Our parents give us life, but it's up to us to choose our way of life.

So, are you just going through life or growing through it? Let's choose growth, gratitude, and a dash of humour along the way. After all, life's too short to be anything but awesome!

Cheers to making every waking hour count!

What's your confidence treasure?

Often, our past achievements are a source of confidence. They're success stories demonstrating that we have done it in the past and can do it now as well.

We do hear about having vision boards, but what we can also have alongside our vision boards is our success board.

Success board pulls us up on our low days.

Success board is our source of confidence.

Here's how to make the most of a success board:

Gather a list of your achievements, whether big or small. This could be closing a significant deal, successfully leading a project, or even a moment of personal growth. Every success counts.

Create a visual board–either physical or digital–where you can display these successes. Include photos, certificates, or even positive feedback from colleagues and clients.

Keep your success board dynamic by revising it every few months. Add recent wins to keep it current and relevant. This continuous process ensures that your board grows with you, reflecting your ongoing journey of success.

Place your success board where you can see it daily. Let it be a source of motivation and a reminder of your potential. On tough days, a glance at your board can reignite your confidence and drive.

Don't hesitate to share your success board with your team. Encourage them to create their own. This not only builds individual confidence but fosters a culture of recognition and appreciation within your organisation.

By integrating a success board into your routine, you're not just acknowledging your past achievements; you're actively reinforcing your belief in your capabilities.

Let your success board pull you up on low days and propel you towards future successes with unwavering confidence.

Start building yours today and watch your self-assurance soar!

How fast are you running in this race?

As any seasoned planter or farmer will tell you, slow growth leads to dense and hard wood in trees. These trees, although they take their time, develop strength and resilience that fast-growing ones simply can't match.

In today's fast-paced world, it's easy to get caught up in the rush for quick success. But just as with trees, speeding things up in our professional lives can sometimes do more harm than good.

Building a successful career is a lifelong game, and it's crucial to invest in ourselves, take the time to learn, and grow at a sustainable pace.

Much like slow-growing trees, marathon runners train methodically over time, gradually building their endurance. They don't sprint through every practice session; instead, they balance their workouts with periods of rest and recovery.

This deliberate pace ensures they avoid injury and burnout, ultimately leading them to cross the finish line with strength and stamina.

Remember, slow growth might seem less glamorous, but it fosters deep-rooted strength and resilience.

You choose what pace is sustainable for you and go by that.

Concluding Remarks

As you reach the end of this book, I'd like to say that just start somewhere. Start with a habit that aligns with your life goals and give it time—give your new habit time to take root, be consistent with it, and watch the results unfold over time.

Do not be outcome-focused, instead be input driven—for example, to cultivate a reading habit, do not have an inflexible goal of reading one book per week or month, because if you're unable to stick to it, you'll end up quitting. Rather, have a goal of reading for just five to ten minutes each day.

Start small, and then gradually grow big. Take baby steps in the direction of transformation. Picking up this book and reading it was one step. Congratulate yourself for completing it. Now, take the next thoughtful step and pick a habit. Break it down to fit it in your existing routine and grow from there.

If you have benefited even slightly from reading this book—even 1%, keep that 1% consistent, because over time you'll see the compound effect of that 1% improvement. Small, incremental improvements may seem insignificant in the short term, but their impact multiplies over time, leading to substantial growth and transformation.

Pass this knowledge to someone else as well, because the more you empower and teach others what you know, the better you get at it.

Thank you for taking the time to read this book. I hope it has provided you with valuable insights and practical strategies for building healthy habits. Remember, the journey of a thousand miles begins with a single step. Make that step today and watch how your life transforms over time.

Acknowledgements

WRITING this book has been a journey filled with learning, growth, and support from many incredible individuals. I would like to take a moment to express my deepest gratitude to those who have made this book possible.

First and foremost, I want to thank my family. To my husband, Rohit, your unwavering support and encouragement have been my anchor throughout this process. Thanks for creating an environment and space for me to write and for covering up for my absence on multiple occasions. To my daughter, Aarna, thank you for being my inspiration and for your patience and understanding during the countless hours I spent writing. My in-laws Sudesh Saini and Nutan Saini, for understanding my working weekends. My mother Rajni, brother Karunesh, and sister-in-law Lakshmi, thanks for being the pillar for me in times of need and always encouraging my creative expression.

I am deeply grateful to my editor, Debasmita Dutta, whose keen insights and meticulous attention to detail have significantly improved the quality of this book. Your guidance has been invaluable.

A special thanks to my literary agent, Navya and her entire team, for believing in this project from the very beginning and for your tireless efforts in bringing it to fruition.

I would like to acknowledge the countless mentors and advisors who have shaped my thinking and provided invaluable feedback. Your wisdom and experience have been a guiding light through my dilemmas and pushing me to my limits.

This book would not have been possible without the contributions of numerous researchers and authors whose work has inspired and informed my own.

Shireen, thanks for bringing this book to life—you know why. If it weren't for you, this book would still be sitting on my desktop. Thanks for being there whenever I needed.

Finally, I want to thank you, the readers. Your curiosity and passion for better habits have driven me to write. I hope this book provides you with valuable insights and inspires you to embark on your own journey of discovery and growth.

References

1. '10 Benefits of Rising Early, and How to Do It.' Zen Habits. https://zenhabits.net/10-benefits-of-rising-early-and-how-to-do-it/.
2. '10 Reasons to Learn Something New Everyday.' The GoodLife Centre. https://www.thegoodlifecentre.co.uk/10-reasons-to-learn-something-new-everyday/.
3. '20+ Health Benefits of Meditation According to Science.' PositivePsychology.Com. Jeremy Sutton, June 19, 2019. https://positivepsychology.com/benefits-of-meditation/.
4. '8 Health Benefits of Exploring New Places.' Push Doctor. https://www.pushdoctor.co.uk/exercise/8-health-benefits-of-exploring-new-places.
5. '9 Benefits of Yoga.' Johns Hopkins Medicine. https://www.hopkinsmedicine.org/health/wellness-and-prevention/9-benefits-of-yoga.
6. '9 Reasons to Get Up Early.' Healthline. https://www.healthline.com/health/healthy-sleep/benefits-of-waking-up-early#benefits.

7. 'Balancing Work and Life: Embracing Digital Detox in the Modern Workplace.' Great Place to Work. November 30, 2023. https://www.greatplacetowork.in/balancing-work-and-life-embracing-digital-detox-in-the-modern-workplace.

8. 'Benefits of Physical Activity.' Physical Activity Basics. April 24, 2024. https://www.cdc.gov/physical-activity-basics/benefits/index.html.

9. 'Diet and Mental Health: How Nutrition Shapes Your Well-Being.' McleanHospital.Org. May 24, 2024. https://www.mcleanhospital.org/essential/nutrition.

10. 'Exercise & Fitness.' Harvard Health Publishing. September 27, 2024. https://www.health.harvard.edu/topics/exercise-and-fitness.

11. 'Food and Mental Health.' Mind. https://www.mind.org.uk/information-support/tips-for-everyday-living/food-and-mental-health/.

12. 'Giving Thanks Can Make You Happier.' Harvard Health Publishing. August 14, 2021. https://www.health.harvard.edu/healthbeat/giving-thanks-can-make-you-happier.

13. 'Health Benefits of Cleaning.' RUSH. https://www.rush.edu/news/health-benefits-cleaning.

14. 'Healthy Diet.' World Health Organization. https://www.who.int/initiatives/behealthy/healthy-diet.

15. 'Kindness Is Good for Mental Health and Overall Well-being.' Barnstable County. November 13, 2023. https://www.capecod.gov/2023/11/13/kindness-is-good-for-mental-health-and-overall-well-being/.

16. 'Mental Health Benefits of Journaling.' WebMD. February 25, 2024. https://www.webmd.com/mental-health/mental-health-benefits-of-journaling.

17. "No Age for Learning': Inside India's School for the Elderly.' BBC News India. September 13, 2024. Video, https://www.youtube.com/watch?v=hU0myuPljMI.

18. 'Practicing Gratitude.' NIH News In Health. https://newsinhealth.nih.gov/2019/03/practicing-gratitude.

19. 'Solar-powered Tuk-tuk Completes India to UK Trip.' BBC News. September 16, 2016. Video, https://www.bbc.com/news/av/world-asia-india-37389181.

20. 'The Benefits of Listening to Music.' Healthline. https://www.healthline.com/health/benefits-of-music#community-benefits.

21. 'The Benefits of Waking Up Early: Enhancing Mental Health and Overall Well-being.' Integrative Psych. Integrative Psych, October 8, 2018. https://www.integrative-psych.org/resources/the-benefits-of-waking-up-early-enhancing-mental-health-and-overall-well-being.

22. 'The Fine Art of Listening Can Transform the Quality of Your Communication and Relationships.' MentalHealth.Com. September 25, 2024. https://www.mentalhealth.com/library/the-art-of-listening-in-relationships.

23. 'The Importance of Digital Detox: Reclaiming Your Time and Focus.' Pegasus Communication Solutions. October 9, 2024. https://www.pcsvoip.com/the-importance-of-digital-detox-reclaiming-your-time-and-focus/.

24. 'The Power of Affirmations.' Louise Hay. https://www.louisehay.com/the-power-of-affirmations/.

25. 'The Power of Why: How Asking the Right Questions Can Change the Future.' Performance Excellence Network. February 23, 2021. https://performanceexcellencenetwork.org/pensights/the-power-of-why-how-asking-the-right-questions-can-change-the-future-feb-2021/.

26. 'What Does Clutter Do to Your Brain and Body?' NewsGP. January 25, 2019. https://www1.racgp.org.au/newsgp/clinical/what-does-clutter-do-to-your-brain-and-body.

27. 'Yoga: How Did It Conquer the World and What's Changed?' BBC. June 22, 2017. https://www.bbc.com/news/world-40354525.

28. 'Me-Time Is a Need for Mental Health.' DX Wellness. https://dx-wellness.com/me-time-is-a-need-for-mental-health-2/.

29. Andersen, Isabella. 'Why Taking Risks Is Good For You.' Project Happiness. May 16, 2022. https://shop.projecthappiness.org/blogs/project-happiness/why-taking-risks-is-good-for-you.

30. Asp, Karen. 'How to Claim Some 'Me Time'.' WebMD. https://www.webmd.com/balance/features/prioritizing-time-for-yourself-for-health.

31. Blicharski, Kristi. 'Letting Go and Becoming the CEO of Your Own Happiness.' Tiny Buddha. https://tinybuddha.

com/blog/letting-go-and-becoming-the-ceo-of-your-own-happiness/.

32. Chen, Ying, Jess Haines, Brittany M Charlton, and Tyler J VanderWeele. 'Positive Parenting Improves Multiple Aspects of Health and Well-Being in Young Adulthood.' Nature human behaviour, July 2019. https://pmc.ncbi.nlm.nih.gov/articles/PMC6625866/.
33. Chidambaram, Karthik. 'How Planning Ahead Helps You Maximize Productivity.' KC. February 22, 2023. https://www.karthikchidambaram.com/how-planning-ahead-benefits-your-life/.
34. Clear, James. 'The Science of Developing Mental Toughness in Your Health, Work, and Life.' JamesClear.Com. https://jamesclear.com/mental-toughness.
35. Cooks-Campbell, Allaya. 'Learn Something New Every Day to Enjoy Never-ending Growth.' BetterUp. June 28, 2023. https://www.betterup.com/blog/learn-something-new.
36. Das, Geetali. 'Reading Habit and Its Importance in Society.'
37. https://www.sbmscollege.org/library/faculty-publications/arunav-golden-jubilee-year-pages-88-91.pdf.
38. Ferrari, Joseph. 'Speaking of Psychology: Why Clutter Stresses Us Out.' American Psychological Association. https://www.apa.org/news/podcasts/speaking-of-psychology/clutter.

39. Freeman, Kameshia L. 'The Importance of Asking Why.' LinkedIn. March 22, 2022. https://www.linkedin.com/pulse/importance-asking-why-kameshia-l-freeman/.

40. Gordon, Sherri. 'The Connection Between Cleanliness and Mental Health.' Very Well Mind. April 24, 2024. https://www.verywellmind.com/how-mental-health-and-cleaning-are-connected-5097496.

41. Grevenstein, Dennis, Matthias Bluemke, Jochen Schweitzer, and Corina Aguilar-Raab. 'Better Family Relationships––Higher Well-being: The Connection between Relationship Quality and Health Related Resources.' ScienceDirect. May 15, 2019. https://doi.org/10.1016/j.mph.2019.200160.

42. Hardy, Benjamin. 'The Scientific Argument for Waking Up Early.' Medium. October 8, 2018. https://medium.com/thrive-global/the-scientific-argument-for-waking-up-early-b3d93c4d74cd.

43. Kubicek, Lorrie. 'Can Music Improve Our Health and Quality of Life?' Harvard Health Publishing. July 25, 2022. https://www.health.harvard.edu/blog/can-music-improve-our-health-and-quality-of-life-202207252786.

44. Lufkin, Bryan. 'Is Waking up Early Good or Bad?' BBC. February 14, 2019. https://www.bbc.com/worklife/article/20190213-is-waking-up-early-good-or-bad.

45. Manzano, Perry. 'How to Stay Calm in Frustrating Situations (Even if You Have Zero Patience).' Tiny Buddha. https://tinybuddha.com/blog/how-to-stay-

calm-in-frustrating-situations-even-if-you-have-zero-patience/.

46. Moore, Catherine. 'Positive Daily Affirmations: Is There Science Behind It?' PositivePsychology.Com. March 4, 2019. https://positivepsychology.com/daily-affirmations/.
47. Munoz, Catalina. 'How Asking Questions Changed the Course Of History.' Medium. February 7, 2022. https://catalina-munoz.medium.com/how-asking-questions-changed-the-course-of-history-4af22f6066d9.
48. Neirotti, Rodolfo A. 'The Importance of Asking Questions and Doing Things for a Reason.' National Library of Medicine. https://pmc.ncbi.nlm.nih.gov/articles/PMC7918389/.
49. Nucleus AI. 'The Power of Not Reacting: Buddha's Approach to Peaceful Living.' Your Story. https://yourstory.com/2023/09/buddhas-guide-mastering-emotions.
50. Owen, M M. 'The Art of Listening.' Aeon. May 30, 2022. https://aeon.co/essays/the-psychologist-carl-rogers-and-the-art-of-active-listening.
51. Pham, Quyen. 'Why It's Important to Take Risks to Further Your Career.' Forbes. May 16, 2022. https://www.forbes.com/councils/forbesbusinessdevelopmentcouncil/2022/05/16/why-its-important-to-take-risks-to-further-your-career/.
52. Popkin, Barry M., Kristen E. D'Anci, and Irwin H. Rosenberg. 'Water, Hydration and Health.' *National*

Institutes of Health 68, no. 8 (2010): 439-58. https://pmc.ncbi.nlm.nih.gov/articles/PMC2908954/pdf/nihms210404__1.pdf.

53. Rao, Srinivas. 'Why Planning Your Day the Night Before Drastically Increases Your Productivity.' Medium. January 18, 2017. https://medium.com/the-mission/why-planning-your-day-the-night-before-drastically-increases-your-productivity-5f12c678b384.
54. Rudolph, Kelly. 'Self-Care & The Importance of 'Me-Time'.' Positive Women Rock. https://positivewomenblog.com/self-care-me-time/.
55. Singh, Chandan & REDDY, T. (2020). Yoga Origin, History and Development in India.
56. Smith, Jeremy A. 'How Much Control Do You Have Over Your Own Happiness?' Greater Good Magazine. May 11, 2022. https://greatergood.berkeley.edu/article/item/how_much_control_do_you_have_over_your_own_happiness.
57. Wagstaff, Jackson V. 'Benefits of the Habit of Reading.' *Marriott Student Review 4*, no. 4 (2020). https://scholarsarchive.byu.edu/cgi/viewcontent.cgi?article=1254&context=marriottstudentreview.
58. Weinberg, Robert. (2013). Mental toughness: What is it and how to build it. Revista da Educação Física / UEM. 24. 1-10. 10.4025/reveducfis.v24.1.17523. https://www.researchgate.net/publication/262665458_Mental_toughness_What_is_it_and_how_to_build_it/citation/download

59. Wikipedia. 2024. 'Ajeet Bajaj.' Wikimedia Foundation. Last modified December 28, 2024. https://en.wikipedia.org/wiki/Ajeet_Bajaj.

60. Wikipedia. 2024. 'Harsh Mariwala.' Wikimedia Foundation. Last modified November 15, 2024. https://en.wikipedia.org/wiki/Harsh_Mariwala.

61. Wikipedia. 2024. 'Marie Kondo.' Wikimedia Foundation. Last modified December 24, 2024. https://en.wikipedia.org/wiki/Marie_Kondo.

62. Wise, Abigail. '9 Benefits of Reading Print Books, According to Science.' Real Simple. June 4, 2024. https://www.realsimple.com/health/preventative-health/benefits-of-reading-real-books.

63. Zaraska, Marta. 'Why Being Kind to Others Is Good for Your Health.' BBC. December 16, 2020. https://www.bbc.com/future/article/20201215-why-being-kind-to-others-is-good-for-your-health.

About the Author

Namita Bhalla is a dynamic Chartered Accountant with twelve years of experience who skilfully merges financial expertise with a passion for writing. Beyond her numbers-driven career, she is dedicated to inspiring others through her insights on personal growth, professional development, and the importance of healthy daily habits. Recently, she has taken to LinkedIn to share her journey and empower others.

When she's not balancing budgets or crafting engaging posts, you'll find her enjoying precious moments with her four-year-old daughter, the light of her life. Through her writing, she encourages professionals and individuals to embrace their passions, build resilience, and prioritise well-being. Follow her on LinkedIn for uplifting content, motivation, and a sprinkle of humour!